OECD Reviews of Health Systems

Primary Care in Denmark

OECD

BETTER POLICIES FOR BETTER LIVES

This work is published under the responsibility of the Secretary-General of the OECD. The opinions expressed and arguments employed herein do not necessarily reflect the official views of OECD member countries.

This document and any map included herein are without prejudice to the status of or sovereignty over any territory, to the delimitation of international frontiers and boundaries and to the name of any territory, city or area.

Please cite this publication as:
OECD (2017), *Primary Care in Denmark*, OECD Reviews of Health Systems, OECD Publishing, Paris.
http://dx.doi.org/10.1787/9789264269453-en

ISBN 978-92-64-26944-6 (print)
ISBN 978-92-64-26945-3 (PDF)

Series: OECD Reviews of Health Systems
ISSN 1990-1429 (print)
ISSN 1990-1410 (online)

The statistical data for Israel are supplied by and under the responsibility of the relevant Israeli authorities. The use of such data by the OECD is without prejudice to the status of the Golan Heights, East Jerusalem and Israeli settlements in the West Bank under the terms of international law.

Photo credits: Cover © Halfpoint/Shutterstock.com

Corrigenda to OECD publications may be found on line at: *www.oecd.org/about/publishing/corrigenda.htm*.

Foreword

In many ways, primary care in Denmark performs well. Danish primary care is trusted and valued by patients, and is relatively inexpensive. But there are important areas where it needs to be strengthened. Most critically, Danish primary care is relatively opaque in terms of the performance data available at local level. Greater transparency is vital in the next phase of reform and sector strengthening. Robust information on quality and outcomes empowers patients and gives them choice. It can support GPs to benchmark themselves, and engage in continuous quality improvement. It also allows the authorities to better understand where they should direct additional resources.

This review draws on evidence and best practice from across OECD health systems to support Denmark in agreeing the steps that will strengthen its primary care sector, support it to deliver high-quality, patient-centred care and put it on a sustainable footing as the foundation for a high-performing health system.

ACKNOWLEDGEMENTS

The lead author of this report is Ian Forde. Other authors are Carol Nader, Karolina Socha-Dietrich, Jillian Oderkirk and Francesca Colombo. All authors wish to thank Mark Pearson and Stefano Scarpetta from the OECD's Directorate of Employment, Labour and Social Affairs, as well as the OECD's Economics Department (Denmark desk), for their review of this report and suggestions for improvement. Thanks also go to Lukasz Lech and Isabelle Vallard for editorial assistance.

This report benefited from the expertise and insights of several health system stakeholders met during a mission to Denmark in April 2016. These included officials from the Ministry of Health and the Ministry of Finance; the Danish regions; Local Government Denmark; the Danish Health Authority; the Danish Health Data Authority; the Danish Organisation of General Practitioners; the Danish College of General Practitioners; the Danish Medical Association; the Danish Nurses' Organisation; the Danish General Practice Quality Unit; Danish Patients; and, Professors Flemming Bro, Mickael Bech, Kjeld Møller Pedersen, John Sahl Andersen and Jens Søndergaard.

Particular thanks are due to officials from the Ministry of Health and the Ministry of Finance; the Danish regions; Local Government Denmark and the Danish Organisation of General Practitioners for reviewing earlier drafts and making suggestions to strengthen the report. The authors acknowledge with gratitude the work of Rasmus Fynbo Aagaard-Jensen from the Ministry of Finance for co-ordinating the Danish authorities' input into this report.

Table of contents

Figures

Tables

Assessment and recommendations

Primary care is well-established at the heart of Denmark's health care system

Denmark's 3 500 general practitioners (GPs), nearly all independent contractors, have a long tradition of providing effective first-line health care, often over many years, to their local communities. Patient surveys show that Danes rate their GP care highly (with 91% giving a positive assessment compared to a European Union average of 84% in a recent survey; OECD, 2013). The effectiveness of primary care is demonstrated by the relatively infrequent need for hospitalisation for some (but not all) chronic conditions.

Denmark's primary care sector has also shown itself capable of innovation and reform. The OECD's 2013 review of health care quality in Denmark highlighted the *Danish General Practice Database* (DAMD) as a professionally-led innovation capable of improving care through detailed analysis of primary care activities and outcomes, which is still unusual across OECD countries (OECD, 2013). The capacity for reform is also illustrated by how complex conditions such as diabetes, that were previously treated entirely by hospital specialists, are now increasingly managed within primary care.

The fundamental role that primary care plays in the Danish health care system means that its performance, and its continued evolution to meet population health care needs and expectations, are valid concerns for those who use, and pay for, primary care.

Pressures and challenges continue to evolve – rapidly

The Danish health care system is, however, facing an array of unprecedented pressures. One in six of the population is aged over 65 years – set to grow to one in four by 2050 (OECD Health Statistics, 2016). Although many elderly individuals lead active and fulfilling lives, the increasing prevalence of long-term conditions such as diabetes, arthritis or depression inevitably means more frequent contacts with the health care system. Effective primary and secondary prevention will also be needed to reduce the burden of chronic illness and ensure a healthy, active population.

Much of this workload will fall to primary care. Denmark has been unusually dynamic in reducing the size of its hospital sector. The number of hospital beds has fallen to 3.1 per 1 000 population, considerably less than comparator countries such as Germany (8.3), Finland (4.9) or Norway (3.9). After a heart attack, Danes spend just under four days in hospital before being transferred back to community care – the fastest discharge time in the OECD. Consequently, more is expected of community services, and reforms in 2007 gave municipalities responsibility for providing long-term elderly care, rehabilitation and public health, with GPs (who sign agreements with regional governments), being responsible for providing primary health care.

Given intensifying awareness of the need to improve performance and value for money across all publicly-funded health systems, it is reasonable to ask how Danish primary care is facing up to these challenges. In many respects, as already illustrated, the quality and efficiency of Danish primary care is strong. There are, however, some areas that are notably weak. The most important of these concerns the sector's lack of transparency.

The most urgent issue facing Danish primary care is its lack of transparency

A stark illustration of the lack of transparency concerns collapse of the *Danish General Practice Database* (DAMD). The 2013 OECD *Review of Health Care Quality* in Denmark highlighted DAMD as having substantial potential to drive continuous quality improvements in primary care, through real-time monitoring of health care needs and patient outcomes, as well as patient-oriented interfaces. In September 2014, the DAMD database was deemed not to meet the legal definition for clinical databases, which limits them to disease-specific registers. It was also judged that DAMD did not collect data for "specified, explicit and legitimate purposes", as required by the European Data Protection Directive 95/46. In consequence, DAMD was suspended. The discussion over legality of DAMD coincided with the 2014 round of negotiations on new health agreement between the GPs' professional body (the *Praktiserende Lægers Organisation*, or PLO) and government, during which the PLO strongly opposed sharing DAMD indicators with the authorities in a way that could identify individual practices. Eventually, the DAMD database was deleted except for few disease specific indicators. This represents a major reversal of transparency and public accountability – areas in which the Danish health system had previously been a global leader.

One of the most disappointing aspects of the partial suspension of DAMD was loss of patients' access to their clinical data in the *Sundhedsjournal* (sundhed.dk, or national health register). This is an ambitious initiative which allows patients to see all their health data (including hospital records, medication, test results and allergies) in one place. In addition, *Mine diabetesdata* was a separate portal designed for patients with diabetes. It was intended to pull information from hospitals, GPs and community care on all aspects related to management of diabetes, and included decision aids for patients to encourage self-management. Both initiatives relied upon DAMD for primary care data. The *Mine diabetesdata* initiative no longer operates, as a result of DAMD's dissolution. The *Sundhedsjournal* continues, but without primary care data.

Some concerns about quality and variation in performance persist

Being able to monitor quality and outcomes is important because primary care performance is not always as good as it could be. Despite reassuring figures on hospital admission for heart failure, prescribing for the elderly and management of diabetes (described in Section 2.2), there is room for improvement, for example, on avoiding hospitalisation for other chronic conditions: 46 per 100 000 Danes were hospitalised for asthma and 288 per 100 000 for chronic bronchitis (COPD) in 2013, two conditions where hospitalisation should be rarely needed if primary care is effective. In Sweden, hospitalisation rates for the same two conditions were 50% and 67% those of Denmark (OECD Health Statistics, 2016).

There is also too much variation within Danish primary care – and we do not know why. Rates of avoidable hospitalisation in people aged over 65 vary two-fold across Danish municipalities (from below 40 to above 90 per 1 000 elderly inhabitants), and delays in discharging once people are ready to leave hospital also vary widely, as described in Section 2.3. This may be due, in part, to variations in the quality of hospital care. The effectiveness of local primary care services is, however, undeniably relevant too.

The relationship between GPs and the authorities responsible for overseeing primary care appears to be under strain

It is also of concern that collaboration between Danish GPs and the authorities who fund primary care and who are democratically accountable for its performance appear to be deteriorating. In addition to the loss of DAMD, another illustration concerns arrangements to provide primary care outside of normal office hours in the Capital Region around Copenhagen. In a legitimate attempt to offer continuity of care, expand access and choice, and relieve pressure on hospital emergency departments, regional authorities developed a telephone triage service. This is staffed by nurses, supported by decision-support software. The nurses are supported GPs who take cases referred to them and take calls directly from patients when free to do so. Similar nurse-led triage services are well-established in other OECD health systems, and have been shown to be safe, efficient and acceptable to patients. The PLO, however, advised its members to boycott participation in the service. As described in Section 2.1, more than 70% of calls are answered by nurses and nearly half of all calls are resolved without further referral. The service is struggling, however, to meet patients' expectations in terms of waiting time for connection to a GP for the subset of patients who are referred to one.

From an external perspective, events such as the loss of DAMD and the PLO's refusal to participate in the Copenhagen's out-of-hours primary care service are at best surprising and, at worst, deeply troubling. They represent "red flags" that indicate that the core public service values of accessibility, quality and accountability that are served through good health information need to be much better communicated with all stakeholders in Denmark, including primary care providers, patients and citizens. OECD experience shows that data-rich health care systems can operate in a manner that serves the public interest, whilst protecting privacy and individual autonomy. Progress towards this important goal should not be subverted to sectorial self-interest.

Some municipalities have also struggled to deliver the primary care functions assigned to them

Primary care in Denmark is not entirely in the hands of GPs. As mentioned earlier, reforms in 2007 handed significant responsibilities for the provision of certain health and social care services to Denmark's 98 municipalities. Some municipalities have struggled to fulfil the expectations placed upon them. In particular, waiting times for rehabilitation services are still above the agreed target of 14 days in a number of them. Increases in the number of people being referred for rehabilitation services may partly explain this (and, in some cases, there are clinical reasons for delaying the start of rehabilitation). Nevertheless, it is broadly acknowledged that some municipalities have had difficulties in providing care effectively.

Close co-operation between municipalities and GPs became necessary as a result of the 2007 reforms, to reduce hospital use by avoiding unnecessary admissions and reducing length of stay. Attempts were made to reach local agreements on how primary care services needed to evolve in response to reorganisation of the hospital sector, but few if any effective agreements were reached, as described in Section 1.3. The lack of a system-level approach and additional funds to support the transfer of care to community services also hampered effective local responses to the reorganisation of the hospital sector. As a result, co-operation between municipalities and GPs does not always work well. GPs note, for example, that their participation in planning meetings is impossible if municipalities schedule these mid-morning when GPs are seeing patients.

Over time, however, the partnership between GPs and municipalities is reportedly becoming more effective. An illustration of this is the recent agreement (in May 2016) to focus on improving the quality of long-term care and reducing hospital admissions among elderly. Although an initiative of national government, this agreement is based upon an understanding of close co-operation between GPs and municipality services. Transparency on comparative performance, identifying and sharing best practice and supporting poor performers will be critical to improving primary care for the vulnerable elderly.

What steps should government, clinicians and patients take to ensure that Danish primary care delivers best value?

The national contract specifying GPs' activities, ways of working and remuneration is about to be renegotiated. Now is a good moment, therefore, to identify the critical steps that need to be taken to ensure that accessibility, quality and accountability remain at the heart of Danish primary care.

The basis for such an agreement should be population health care needs and expectations. There is no disagreement over the most important issues here: population ageing and more prevalent ageing and long-term conditions, accompanied by the expectation of care closer to home or at home (that is, hospitalisation only where care cannot be provided in another way). Co-ordination and continuity of care for those with complex needs are also indispensable.

Likewise, there is consensus on the broad characteristics of the service model needed. There is agreement that a specialist, adequately resourced primary care sector should be front and centre of the health system's response to evolving health care needs and expectations. There is also agreement that primary care will need some integration (with respect to clinical and organisational data, communications and workforce) with other parts of the health and social care system to deliver what is expected of it. And because primary care is publicly funded, transparent performance monitoring and accountability need to be in place.

Within this broad consensus, however, considerable disagreement on the details persists. Regarding performance monitoring, for example, the PLO and authorities disagree on what data should be collected, who should own it, and how it should be analysed and used. Regarding value for money, the PLO and authorities disagree on how much funding primary care should receive, and the on the mechanisms and incentives that should underpin disbursement to primary care providers. There is also disagreement on how service models (with respect to care outside of normal office hours, for example) and employment models (with respect to advanced nursing roles, for example) should develop.

The aim of this report is to draw on evidence and best practice from across OECD health systems to support Denmark in agreeing the steps that will strengthen its primary care sector, support it to deliver high-quality, patient-centred care and put it on a sustainable footing as the foundation for a high-performing health system. The fundamental principle underpinning the report's recommendations is that the patient's needs and expectations should come first and guide all other actors.

Greater transparency on the quality and outcomes achieved in primary care is Denmark's most urgent need

A rich information infrastructure is the fundamental platform that underpins nearly every other initiative to improve health system performance and sustainability. Danish primary care had this. Its loss, through the near-total suspension and deletion of the DAMD database, was a major step backward. Although reasonable concerns triggered debate around the collection and use of primary care data, it is unfortunate that a resolution other than suspension and deletion was not found. Most importantly, patient groups in Denmark have called for DAMD's restitution.

There have been moves to restore DAMD, but this is happening in a piecemeal fashion by adding primary care data from a small number of groups, with specific diagnoses, to clinical quality databases. Such an approach is squarely antithetical to the spirit and purpose of primary care – which seeks to provide holistic, person-centred care rather than disease-specific care. It is also unclear how a DAMD reconstituted in this way would serve the needs of patients with multiple diagnoses, or no diagnosis at all but nevertheless in need of primary care (such as the young or frail).

Denmark should take steps to further develop national governance of personal health data. This should permit collection, analysis and public reporting of data on primary care performance. This requires data that is not fragmented into distinct silos relating to specific diagnostic groups. Information systems capable of reflecting the reality of complex, multi-morbidity is fundamental to evaluating its quality and the outcomes of primary care, given the increasing numbers of patients with more than one chronic condition. National governance must protect – and be seen to protect – patients' privacy while, at the same time, enabling critical data to be used to drive continuously improving health care, thus serving the public interest.

Restitution of DAMD will allow demonstration of the outcomes and value achieved in primary care. In particular, reporting the outcomes achieved in the prevention and management of chronic disease should be prioritised. Benchmarking at individual practice level should also become standard, to identify excellence, support poorer performers and reduce variation. DAMD was previously strong in these areas, allowing GPs to compare control of blood pressure, cholesterol, glycaemia and nephropathy in their diabetic patients over time and with other practices, for example, and so this should not be a new challenge for Denmark. It is promising that the PLO reports exploring seven new indicators of primary care quality, which could be used to benchmark individual practitioners against their peers.

As well as rebuilding capacity in these areas, future development of DAMD should prioritise collection of patient experience measures and patient-reported outcome measures, particularly those that can be benchmarked internationally. Several OECD health systems report patient experience data in primary care at annual or other regular intervals, whereas the DANPEP survey of general practice patients in Denmark is neither systematic (across all regions) or regular. Patient experience data should also be reported in a way that is comparable internationally. Sweden, Norway and 17 other primary care systems benchmark patient satisfaction through the OECD's *Health Care Quality Indicators* project, but Denmark is not one of them. Work to harmonise these indicators should be undertaken, otherwise Denmark loses the opportunity to compare its performance against other OECD health systems, a benefit it enjoys for nearly every other health care quality indicator.

Richer performance data will allow primary care funding to be better linked to quality and outcomes

The way primary care services are paid for is still dominated by fee-for-service (FFS) in Denmark. Traditional FFS is well suited to discrete activities that can be defined precisely and that have a natural limit to demand, such as vaccination. They are less suited for more the complex or continuous activities, such as health promotion, prevention and co-ordination of care for chronic diseases, which characterise the bulk of modern primary care. The FFS schedule used in Danish primary care has undergone only marginal reform in recent years. Fees can still be earned for imprecise activities such as "blood test", or "preventive counselling", which are not linked to the patient's needs or any specified outputs. This makes it hard to understand exactly what is being done and to reward value appropriately. The urgency of better understanding primary care activity is illustrated by the 36% decline in primary care preventive activity between 2006 and 2014 reported by Statistics Denmark, at a time when chronic disease burden is high and poised to rise further.

Furthermore, fees are constant in real terms. Any productivity gains, for example by shifting some tasks to nurses, do not translate into lower fees and relative gains are kept by the GP. In addition, the relative size of the fees remains constant over time. This means that changes in the relative fees cannot be used to promote for example better disease management of chronically ill patients, instead of more consultations.

In contrast, primary care systems in other OECD countries have taken a more ambitious approach to reforming FFS schedules. In Japan, for example, where the health system is entirely funded by FFS, the notion of a "service" has been considerably developed. Activities in the FFS schedule oriented toward primary care include setting up co-ordinated community care plans upon a patient's discharge; setting-up cancer care plans; and providing co-ordinated management plans for patients with two or more of hypertension, diabetes, dyslipidaemia or dementia.

Other countries have developed FFS into "bundled payment" systems. Bundled payments can be considered to sit somewhere between FFS and risk-adjusted capitation schemes. They pay for a package of care for a defined population with complex care needs, over a specific time period. The Netherlands, for example, has a decade's experience with bundled payments for two diabetes, COPD and cardiovascular disease risk management in primary care. The bundled payment for diabetes showed improvements in quality. Despite a reduction in the use of specialist care (25%), however, costs increased by EUR 288 per patient per year, the reasons for which are unclear.

Pay for performance (P4P) in primary care also continues to generate interest across OECD health systems. The largest, longest established and most evaluated primary care P4P programme is the United Kingdom's *Quality and Outcomes Framework.* This has been associated with increases in quality and access for incentivised activities (particularly in socioeconomically deprived areas). Impacts on outcomes such as mortality, however, have been modest or absent. Primary care P4P programmes in other countries have found broadly similar results. This underlines the importance of seeing P4P schemes as one element of a well-designed reimbursement and accountability framework, blending different payment mechanisms and non-financial incentives.

Denmark has previously experimented with payment reform. In 2007, a voluntary bundled payment system was introduced for patients with diabetes. This included an annual consultation and the co-ordination of specialist services such as eye care, endocrinology, and podiatry. The payment was set at EUR 156, and replaced the existing capitation and FFS payment of EUR 17 per consultation. Uptake amongst GPs, however, was low (only about 10% of all diabetic patients were covered), possibly because of the level of the bundled payment and concerns about eventual uses of the data. The scheme was discontinued in 2014.

Denmark should resume its exploration of new ways to pay for primary care to optimise paying for quality and value, in the context of changing population health care needs. This means finding the right balance between FFS, capitation and newer models such as bundled payments or P4P. Consultation on the design for a new primary care P4P pilot is in fact underway. This pilot will focus on management of chronic conditions, be voluntary, and be in addition to current reimbursements, rather than replace them. The precise details are yet to be worked out, however. It is important that all parties commit to implementing and learning from this and other initiatives, so that the evolving workload of GPs in managing long-term conditions can be reflected as best as possible in the payment system.

Putting data in the hands of patients will make Danish primary care more patient-centred

To reinforce the patient-centredness of Danish primary care, restoring patients' access to this information should be a priority. There is also an economic argument to do so, since international evidence demonstrates that the health care costs of patients who are active participants in managing their care can be substantially lower than those of patients who are less involved (after controlling for demographics and severity of illness). This imperative to restore patients' ability to interact with their primary care data should accelerate efforts to change the legal framework that authorises clinical registers in Denmark.

Other steps, however, are also needed to ensure that patient's needs and expectations remain fully at the centre of Danish primary care. Allowing patients to see how the quality, outcomes and other performance data of their GP practice compares with that of other practices is another important aspect of transparency that Denmark should work towards. Danish GPs have legitimate concerns that open comparison may not reflect demographic or socioeconomic differences in the contexts within which practices work. This has not held back other health systems from pursuing greater transparency, designing benchmarking tools specifically with patients in mind. Canada's *Your Health System* (yourhealthsystem.cihi.ca), England's *MyNHS* (nhs.uk/service-search/Performance/Search) and Portugal's health service benchmarking website (benchmarking.acss.min-saude.pt) are three particularly sophisticated examples. In each case, contextual differences are dealt with by providing comparators that are physically nearby, organisationally similar, or both.

A richer data infrastructure will also allow more detailed profiling of the practice population – identifying patients with intense resource needs in particular. In most cases, GPs already know who these patients are. It is important, though, that local and national authorities also have a detailed and accurate picture of these patients. This will allow additional support and resources to be directed where they are most needed.

Further innovations in service models and professional roles also have the potential to deliver more patient-centred primary care

Although the extent and complexity of problems dealt with in primary care is now much greater than ever before, the basic model through which primary care is delivered in Denmark remains unchanged. A doctor continues to manage most patient contacts, often working single-handedly (or in a partnership with at most one or two other doctors), assisted by a nurse for traditional nursing activities (such as vaccination or wound care). This model broadly serves Denmark well and remains popular and trusted by patients.

As the health system continues to pivot away from hospital-based care, however, and as expectations of closer integration with other services increase, exploration of variants on the traditional model of primary care may be worthwhile. Primary care services in some OECD countries are evolving to include multi-disciplinary group practices or networks (where GPs work alongside other allied health personnel, such as hospital doctors, dental professionals, pharmacists, clinical psychologists or podiatrists); or multi-sectoral group practices or networks (where GPs also work alongside specialists from fields beyond clinical care, such as long-term care, social welfare, training and employment, or criminal justice). Denmark has taken steps in this direction, with the creation of *Sundhedshuse* (or "Health Houses") in some municipalities, as described in Section 1.3. Early evaluations do not suggest substantially improved inter-professional collaboration, however, signalling the need for further efforts to bring about multi-disciplinary primary care. Closer collaboration between GPs and social workers and nurses involved in home care would be particularly beneficial, as health services continue to explore delivering a greater range of services in peoples' homes as part of the increasingly complex pathway of care.

Such models can offer a more comprehensive and integrated response to population health care needs. They typically need changes in payment and incentive structures to support them. The province of Ontario in Canada has undergone a particularly extensive transformation in this regard, and illustrates what is possible. In response to concerns regarding a shortage of GPs, difficulties in access during evenings and weekends and poor integration with other parts of the health system, Ontario began a series of primary care reforms in the late 1990s. The authorities introduced a menu of new service delivery models, allowing GPs to opt for the model that suited them best. In most cases, the models encouraged GPs to form networks of at least three partners, sharing patient lists and clinical records, without necessarily being co-located. "Family Health" interdisciplinary teams and Nurse Practitioner-led clinics were also introduced. New payment models, employing various combinations of FFS, capitation, P4P, and salaries, accompanied the reforms. The new service models have proved popular with Ontario GPs: while in 1998, almost 100% were paid by traditional FFS, this had dropped to around 30% by 2013 (OECD, 2016a).

Experience in Ontario and elsewhere also signals how more could be made of the nursing role. The activities of Denmark's 10 000 primary care nurses (not including health and social care assistants) remain relatively undeveloped compared to other Nordic countries, the Netherlands or England. Danish nurses are not allowed to prescribe, for example, despite the fact that almost all municipalities reportedly want nurses to be able to and the fact that nurse prescribing is well-established in other OECD health systems. More generally, there is very little post-graduate nurse training available in Denmark. This means that even though the FFS schedule in theory allows nurses to take on some tasks traditionally performed by doctors, such task-substitution rarely occurs and innovative service delivery models are held back.

Development of the nursing profession an important priority therefore, which can draw from substantial international experience and which has significant potential to transform primary care. Initial steps would include allowing nurses to prescribe medicines that can be bought over-the-counter, and setting up more nurse-led clinics focussed on preventive health care and health promotion for selected patient groups. Over the longer term, nurse-led clinics for the management of patients with some chronic diseases should be pursued, as already happens in England and other OECD health systems. The *Dansk Sygeplejeråd*, or Danish Nurses' Organization, should take a more proactive role here than it has in the past. Although the Danish Health Authority will ultimately need to authorise any substantial evolution in nursing activity, the Nurses' Organisation can nevertheless lead the agenda by developing short training courses (or longer Masters programmes), and developing their own guidelines and protocols for extended practice.

Once again, better data and transparency will be crucial to any evolution of profession roles. Better understanding of the time GPs spend monitoring stable patients should enable a share of these patients to be transferred to nurses, freeing GPs to concentrate on more complex cases.

Conclusions and policy recommendations

In many ways, primary care in Denmark performs well. Danish primary care is trusted and valued by patient, and is relatively inexpensive. It achieves some good high-level outcomes, such as low hospital admission rates for asthma (although admission rates for other chronic diseases such as diabetes compare less favourably with peers). But there are important areas where it needs to be strengthened. Most importantly, Danish primary care is relatively opaque in terms of the performance data available at local level, in comparison with the hospital sector or primary care systems in other countries.

Greater transparency is critical. Robust and comparable information on quality and outcomes empowers patients and gives them choice. It can support GPs to benchmark themselves and engage in continuous quality improvement. It also allows the authorities to better understand where they should direct additional resources and support, and to plan better. Linking quality and outcomes data to robust data on health care needs, activities and costs and outcomes also allows the relevant authorities to assure value for money. There can be no debate here – publicly-funded services across OECD countries are all pursuing ever greater transparency in performance monitoring and accountability.

Danish primary care has a solid, highly professional and motivated base, and no major changes to its broad configuration are called for. Instead, a number of targeted reforms are needed to support it to deliver high-quality, sustainable, patient-centred care. These include changes to the way that performance data is collected and used, innovations in the way that primary care is paid for and exploration of new professional roles. Service models that reflect deeper integration between primary care and hospital services on the one hand, and primary care and municipality-led services will also lead to more patient-centred care. Key recommendations for the next phase of reform of Danish primary care are set out in the box below.

Substantial international experience is available to guide Denmark in these reforms. The fundamental guiding principle, however, must be that the patient's needs and expectations come first. This foundation should motivate patients, clinicians and managers not to be conservative, but to grasp the opportunity for reform and renew their capacity for innovation and adaptation.

Policy recommendations to strengthen the performance of primary care in Denmark

Ensuring that specialist primary care continues to deliver and demonstrate value, and remains capable of evolving to meet changing patient needs and expectations, requires reforms to:

1. Continuously improve the effectiveness and productivity of primary care, by:

- **Publishing more measures of the outcomes achieved in primary care**, particularly those relating to the management of chronic conditions such as diabetes. Specifically, the current suspension of DAMD should be solved through changes to Danish law, removing the requirement for disease-specific registers and allowing patient-based data collection.
- **Publishing more patient experience measures and patient-reported outcome measures,** particularly those that can be benchmarked internationally. Specifically, the DANPEP survey of patient-experiences in primary care should become systematic, regularly updated, and harmonised with the OECD's *Health Care Quality Indicators.*
- **Encouraging transparency at individual practice level,** to identify excellence, support poorer performers and reduce variation. The Danish authorities should work with GPs to agree on how best to interpret and present differences in performance due to case-mix or other contextual factors, drawing on the approaches developed in Canada, England and other OECD health systems.

2. Innovate in how primary care services are paid for, by:

- **Developing the fee-for-service schedule** to include new items that define more precisely the activities and outcomes to be achieved for specific patient groups. Relative fees for existing service within the schedule should also be varied, to better incentivise high-value care.

Policy recommendations to strengthen the performance of primary care in Denmark *(cont.)*

- **Extending pay-for-performance pilots**, by working with GPs to identify the best mix of fee-for-service (including bundled payments), capitation, pay-for-performance and non-financial incentives to strengthen primary care, with a particular focus on the prevention and treatment of long-term conditions.

- **Piloting other models of payment, such as bundled-payments for patients with complex, chronic disease.** This would build upon Denmark's 2007 experiment with bundled-payments in primary care, and the experience of the Netherlands and other OECD health systems in this area.

3. Deliver more patient-centred care, by:

- **Restoring patients' access to their own primary care data** in the *Sundhesjournal* and the *Mine diabetesdata* initiative, by restoring DAMD as quickly as possible. This should be accompanied by additional initiatives to develop patients' knowledge, skill, and confidence in managing their long-term conditions, such as shared decision-support tools.

- **Allowing patients to compare the quality and outcomes of their GP practice** with that of other practices, by publishing performance benchmarks in patient-friendly formats.

4. Encourage more innovation in the service model, by:

- **Supporting single-handed GPs to deepen and extend collaboration with other primary care practitioners**, either virtually or in-person. This will enable a greater focus on the needs of the community rather than the individual, and better support preventive care, patient education and out-of-hours care.

- **Developing multi-disciplinary and inter-sectoral primary care teams**, where GPs work alongside other allied health personnel such as clinical psychologists or specialists from fields beyond clinical care, such social welfare, training and employment. Central and regional authorities should support municipalities and GPs to develop these new models, through system-wide initiatives to support, for example, the Chronic Care model.

- **Developing the role of primary care nurses,** by allowing prescribing of over-the-counter medicines, nurse-led prevention clinics and, over time, nurse-led management of patients with stable long-term conditions. The Danish Nurses' Organization should take a lead on developing the appropriate guidelines, protocols and training courses to support this.

Policy recommendations to strengthen the performance of primary care in Denmark *(cont.)*

5. Strengthen the governance around the collection and use of personal health data in primary care, by:

- **Improving transparency and public information** about how personal health data is collected, used, and shared with third parties in the interests of continuously improving health and health care.
- **Articulating, in particular, steps that will be taken to manage risks** to individual privacy during the collection and use of personal health data.
- **Revising, where necessary, Denmark's legal and regulatory framework,** to ensure that privacy and data security are protected, whilst enabling the collection and use of data that serves the public interest by improving health and health care.
- **Drawing upon international best practice and standards**, such as the OECD's eight key health data governance mechanisms, to support the strengthening of data governance (OECD, 2015b).

References

OECD (2016a), *Better Ways to Pay for Health Care*, OECD Publishing, Paris, http://dx.doi.org/10.1787/9789264258211-en.

OECD (2016b), *OECD Reviews of Health Care Quality: United Kingdom 2016: Raising Standards*, OECD Publishing, Paris, http://dx.doi.org/10.1787/9789264239487-en.

OECD (2013), *OECD Reviews of Health Care Quality: Denmark 2013: Raising Standards*, OECD Publishing, Paris, http://dx.doi.org/10.1787/9789264191136-en.

Database references

OECD Health Statistics 2016, http://dx.doi.org/10.1787/health-data-en.

Chapter 1

Health Care needs and organisation of primary care in Denmark

Primary care in Denmark faces a number of challenges resulting from increased specialisation in the hospital sector, which translates into shorter inpatient stays and earlier discharge to community care. There has also been a rise in the number of elderly patients with multiple long-term conditions, requiring safe and effective co-ordination of care. The organisational response to these challenges has been relatively slow, however, leaving open questions about how to ensure co-ordination of care, and the central role of general practitioners (GPs) in driving continuous quality improvements.

The statistical data for Israel are supplied by and under the responsibility of the relevant Israeli authorities. The use of such data by the OECD is without prejudice to the status of the Golan Heights, East Jerusalem and Israeli settlements in the West Bank under the terms of international law.

1.1. The socioeconomic context for primary care in Denmark

Denmark is a high-income country with a universal health system funded largely through taxation. The country is divided into five regions, and 88% of the 5.6 million inhabitants live in urban areas (World Bank, 2016).

Denmark is one of the OECD's highest spenders on health care, which accounts for 10.6% of gross domestic product (GDP). This puts Denmark above the OECD average of 9.0%. Government expenditure accounts for 84% of this spending. This proportion is the same as in Sweden (84%) and Norway (85%), and Iceland (82%) but higher than Finland (76%). In consequence, out-of-pocket spending, at 14% of total currently health expenditure, is substantially lower than in the OECD average of 20% (OECD Health Statistics, 2016).

Identifying the primary care sector in national health accounts in a consistent way across different health systems is challenging. Using one definition comprising all "*generalist, outpatient care* (that is, excluding specialist outpatient care and dental care), *home-based care, ancillary services* and *preventive services*" provided in the *ambulatory setting*, Denmark spends around 9% of total current health expenditure on primary care. This estimate is similar to that reported in a recent analysis, namely 9.9% of total health care expenditure in 2012 (Christensen et al., 2016). This figure is more than Norway (6%), but less than the Netherlands (13%), Finland (12%), Sweden and Iceland (both 11%), as well as the OECD average of 12% (Figure 1.1). Widening the definition to include preventive services in *any* setting, brings Denmark's primary care expenditure up to 16% of total current health expenditure, again less than the OECD average of 22%. Including pharmaceuticals adds around 4% to the Danish figure, for both the narrow and wide formulations. With or without pharmaceuticals, in all formulations primary care expenditure in Denmark appears modest compared to other OECD health systems (OECD Health Statistics, 2016).

Figure 1.1. Estimates of primary care spend as a share of total current health expenditure, 2013 (or nearest year)

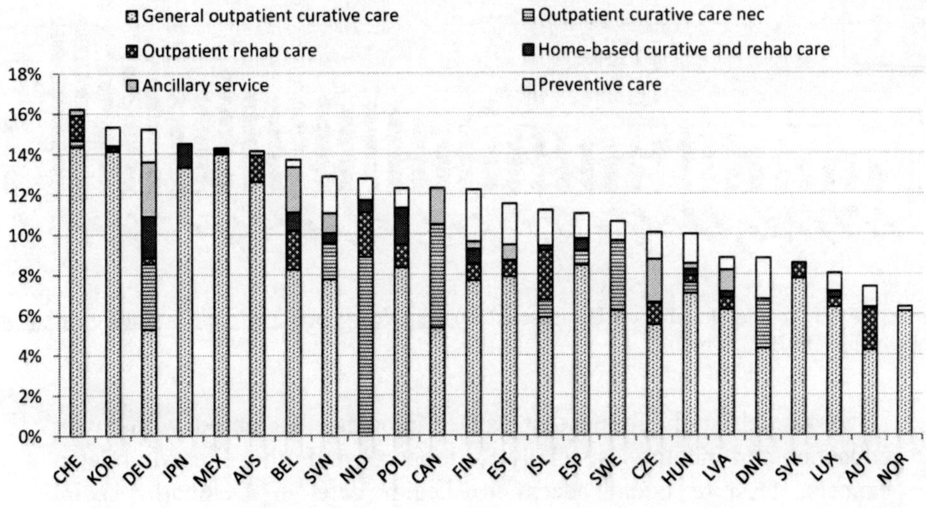

Source: OECD Health Statistics 2016, http://dx.doi.org/10.1787/health-data-en.

The principle of equity is enshrined in the Health Act, which states that citizens should have equal access to health care irrespective of their economic means. Hospital and GP services are free at the point of care for Danish people.

Yet socioeconomic inequalities persist in the country, and – despite the existence of universal health care – these distal factors have some influence on health outcomes. Denmark's poverty rate, at 5.4% using international benchmarks, is low compared with an OECD average of 11.2% (OECD, 2015a). By contrast, the poverty rate for those aged 18 to 25 was much higher at 21.7%, compared with an OECD average of 13.8% (OECD, 2015a), although this is likely to be explained by the large number of students in this age group.

The absolute level of inequality in Denmark, however, is the lowest of all OECD countries (Figure 1.2). Income inequality can be measured by the Gini Coefficient, where 0 equals complete equality and 1 equals complete inequality. The Gini coefficient in Denmark was 0.25 in 2013, well below the OECD average of 0.32 (OECD, 2015a).

Figure 1.2. Income inequality in OECD countries: Gini coefficient, 2007 and 2014

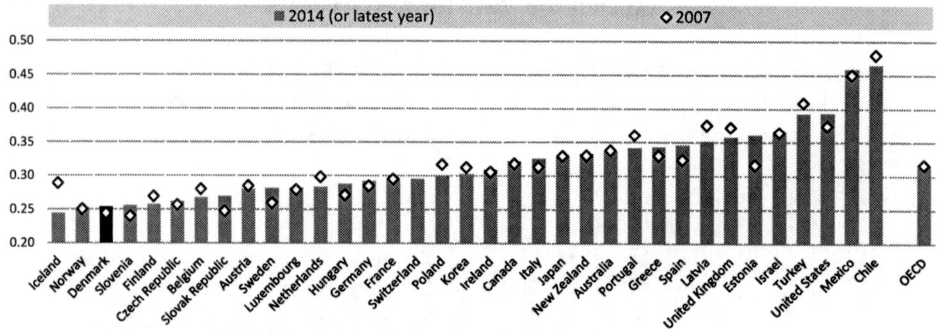

Source: OECD Income Distribution Database (IDD), http://www.oecd.org/social/income-distribution-database.htm; OECD (2016).

A Danish study found that cancer incidence increased with lower education and income, especially for tobacco- and other lifestyle-related cancers. Despite equal access to health care in Denmark, social inequality in the prognosis of most cancers was also observed, marked by poorer relative survival (Dalton et al., 2008). This highlights the need to strengthen health literacy of more marginalised populations, to reduce the behaviours that elevate the risk of cancers and also to educate people as to the importance of early diagnosis to improve case fatality rates.

Further evidence of the impact of social inequalities can be seen in a Danish study conducted in the region of Northern Jutland. It found the risk of mortality varies across educational levels and is significantly higher for those from lower socioeconomic areas. Even when adjusting for behavioural, psychological, material and social determinants, the risk remains significantly higher for those in the lowest two groups of educational levels when compared with vocational upper secondary education (Ullits et al., 2015).

While Denmark is the least unequal country in the OECD, as measured by its Gini Coefficient, the fact remains that pockets of society are living below the poverty line, and inequalities are affecting population health outcomes. Strengthening primary health care to provide timely, responsive and accessible services close to where people live, particularly in more socially-deprived areas, is an important way to keep people healthy and out of more expensive hospital services.

1.2. Health care needs of the Danish population

Denmark faces complex and challenging health care needs related to an increasing burden of complex, chronic disease. This will be accentuated by the demographic transition towards and older population that the country is undergoing. Particularly worrying are increasing rates of non-communicable diseases. Given the increase in obesity and other risk factors, there is little reason to hope that these adverse trends can be reversed in the middle term.

Although life expectancy is improving, Denmark still trails its OECD peers

At 80.8 years, Denmark's life expectancy at birth hovers just above the OECD average of 80.6 (Figure 1.3). This marks an improvement of 7.4 years since 1970. However, Danish life expectancy remains lower than that of Nordic peers Iceland, Sweden, Norway and Finland. In addition, the improvement in Danish life expectancy has progressed at a slower rate than that of the other Nordic countries (OECD Health Statistics, 2016).

Figure 1.3. Life expectancy at birth, 1970 and 2013 (or nearest years)

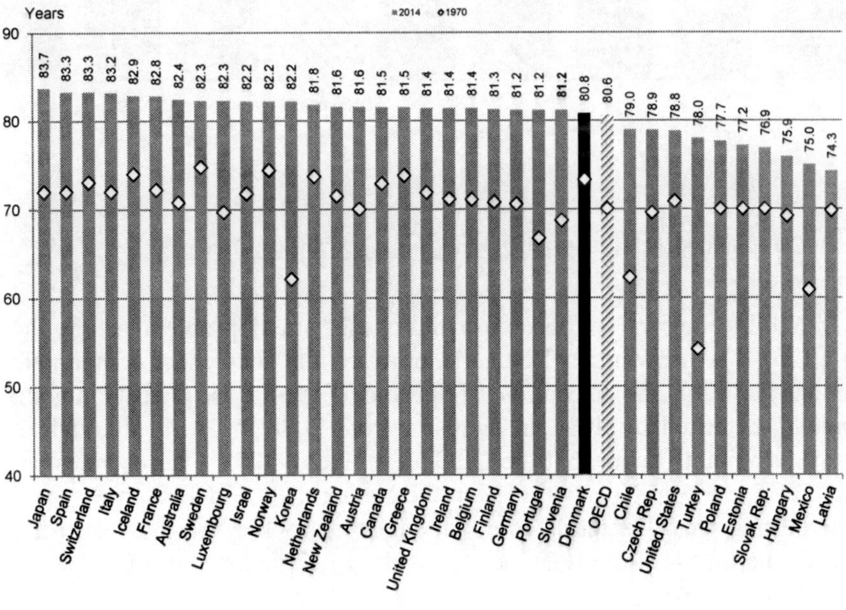

Source: OECD Health Statistics 2016, http://dx.doi.org/10.1787/health-data-en.

This lower life expectancy may be partly explained by higher prevalence of risk factors and chronic disease in the country. For example, Denmark experienced a 44% decline in tobacco consumption, from 30.5% in 2000 to 17% in 2014. While this is a commendable effort, a higher proportion of Danish adults continue to smoke compared with adults in other Nordic countries (Figure 1.4). Of particular note are Sweden and Iceland, which have each reduced the rate of smoking to less than 15% of the adult population (OECD Health Statistics, 2016).

Figure 1.4. Change in daily smoking in adults, 2000 and 2014 (or nearest years)

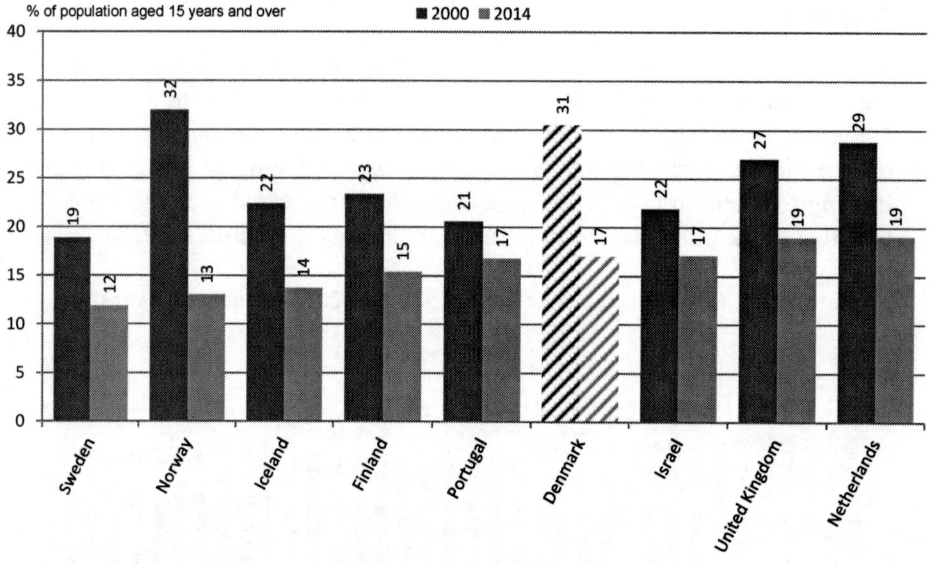

Source: OECD Health Statistics 2016, http://dx.doi.org/10.1787/health-data-en.

While obesity has become a more substantial problem across the OECD, it is growing in Denmark more rapidly than most comparable countries, with the exception of Iceland (Figure 1.5). Obesity among adults increased by 40% in Denmark from 2000 to 2014, although at 15% it remains lower that the OECD average of 17%. Obesity rates are as low as 10% in Norway, 11% in the Netherlands and 12% in Sweden, suggesting that Denmark could do more to tackle this public health epidemic that is strongly associated with type 2 diabetes (OECD Health Statistics, 2016).

Figure 1.5. Increasing obesity among adults in OECD countries, 2000 and 2014 (or nearest years)

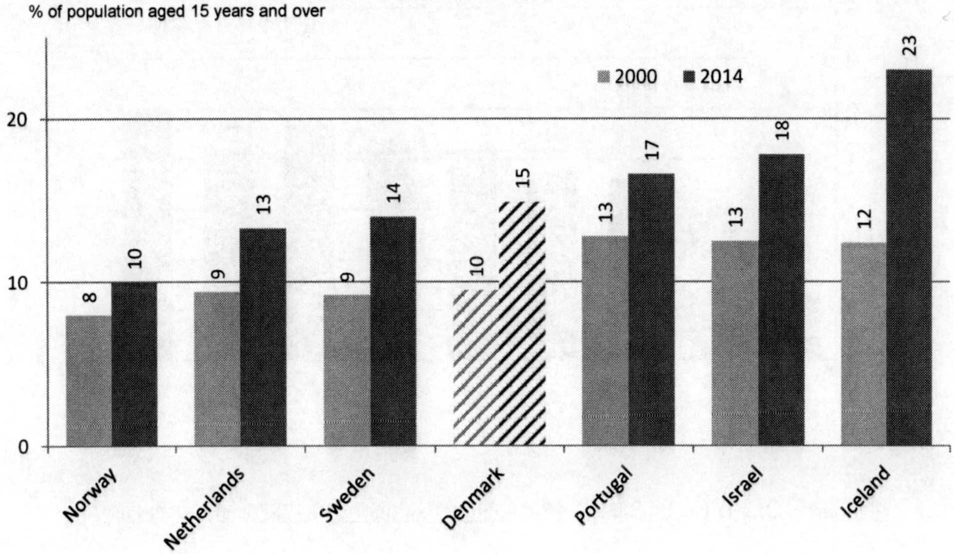

1. Data are based on self-reported height and weight.

Source: OECD Health Statistics 2016, http://dx.doi.org/10.1787/health-data-en.

Another key risk factor for chronic disease is alcohol consumption. While Denmark has experienced the sharpest decline in alcohol consumption compared with its peers, from 13.1 litres per capita per year in 2000 to 9.4 litres in 2014 (Figure 1.6), it continues to have one of the highest rates of alcohol consumption at dangerous levels (Figure 1.7). About 28.5% of the Danish population reported to have engaged in heavy episodic drinking in the previous 30 days. Like all comparable countries, this is much higher among men (37.8%) than women (19.5%; OECD Health Statistics, 2016).

Figure 1.6. Alcohol consumption among adults

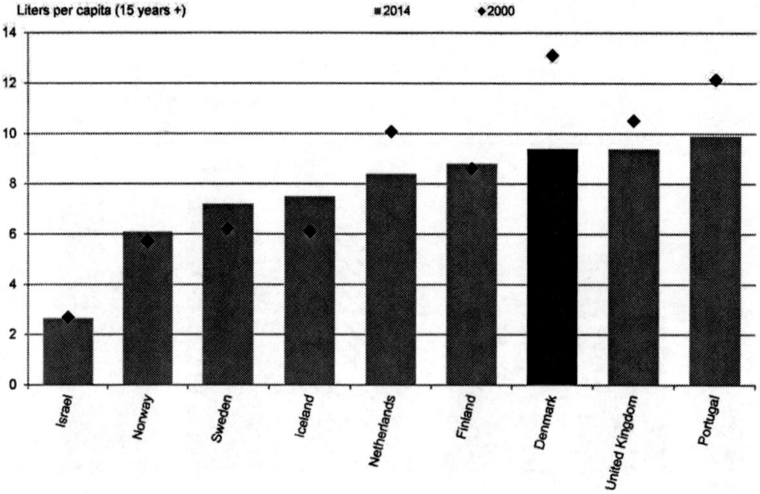

Source: OECD Health Statistics 2016, http://dx.doi.org/10.1787/health-data-en.

Figure 1.7. Heavy episodic drinking, past 30 days, 2010 days 2000 and 2013 (or nearest years)

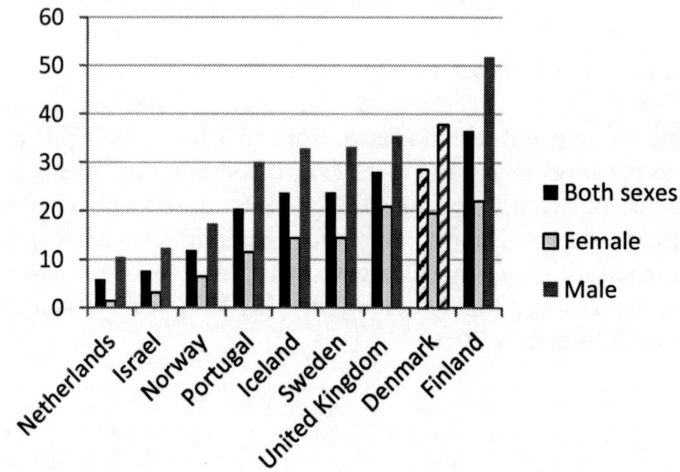

Source: WHO Global Health Observatory data repository, http://dx.doi.org/10.1787/health-data-en.

Poorer health status in Denmark is also reflected in how the Danish population perceives its own health. The proportion of Danish adults who report being in good or very good health declined from 76.6% in 2005 to 72% in 2014 (Figure 1.8). While more Danish adults perceive their health as good or very good compared with the OECD average of 69%, the proportion is lower than most of Denmark's Nordic peers, with the exception of Finland (OECD Health Statistics, 2016).

Figure 1.8. Perceived health status among adults, 2014 (or nearest year)

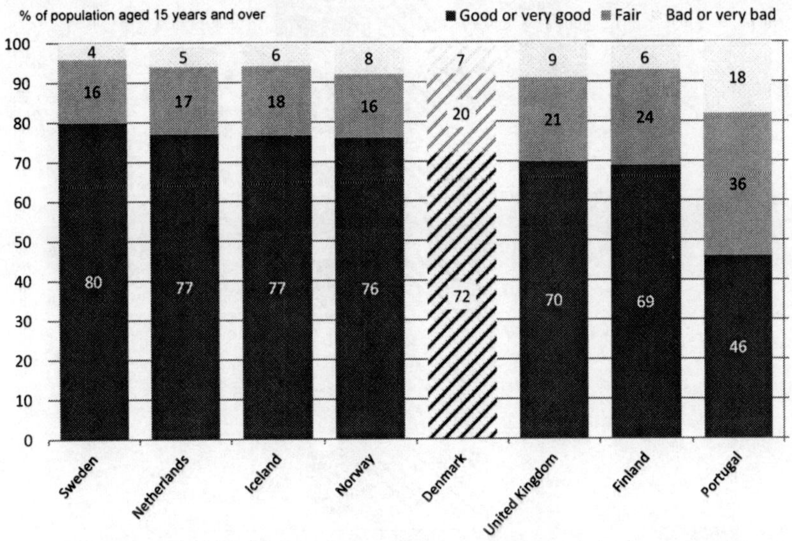

Source: OECD Health Statistics 2016, http://dx.doi.org/10.1787/health-data-en (EU-SILC for European countries).

Denmark's population is rapidly shifting toward an older distribution, and its major health care needs stem from ageing and chronic illnesses

Adding to the challenges facing Denmark's health system is that, in common with many OECD countries, the population is undergoing a rapid transition (Figure 1.9). In 2010, 17% of the country's population was aged 65 and over. By 2050, it is projected that this age group will account for almost one-quarter of the population (OECD Health Statistics, 2016).

Figure 1.9. Share of the population aged 65 years and over, 2010 and 2050

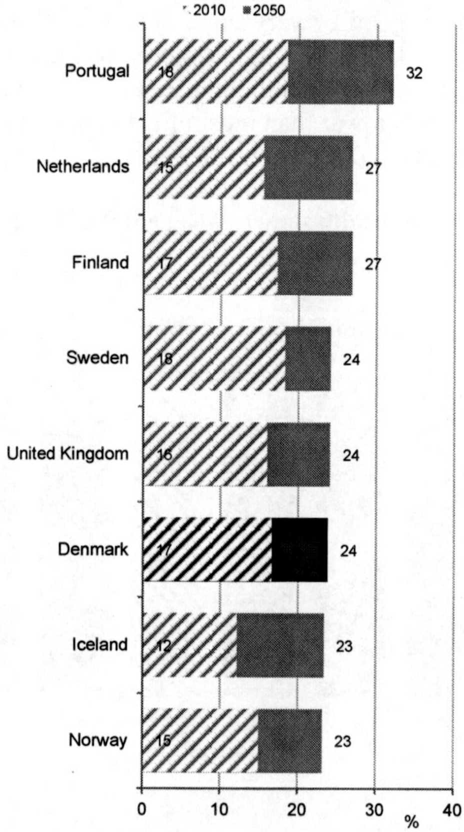

Source: OECD Historical Population Data and Projections Database, 2015.

This ageing trend is associated with more chronic disease, and more multi-morbidity. This means that not only will there be more elderly people with ill health, they are likely to be living with more than one long-term condition. This will create a need to manage more patients with increasing complexity. Adding to this disease burden is improved life expectancy has increased the pool of people living longer with chronic disease. Around one-third of the Danish population has been diagnosed with one or more chronic diseases.

The anticipated need of a more substantial older population will require a focus on strengthening primary care to better manage the burden of chronic disease associated with ageing. This includes a concerted effort to provide care that is better co-ordinated across the care pathway, so that patients can be effectively managed by multidisciplinary teams equipped to respond to all patients' needs. More effective primary and secondary prevention will also be needed. Targeted health promotion in schools, workplaces, other community settings and, where appropriate, peoples' homes will also be vital.

Geographical and socio-economic inequalities in health status also complicate Danish health care needs

The Danish National Health Profile examines the adult population's health, morbidity, wellbeing and use of health services. The survey was conducted in 2010 and 2013, with another due in 2017. It indicates that there are geographical differences and socioeconomic, gender, age and civil status differences in the occurrence of morbidity and lifestyle risk factors. The data are used to draw attention to social inequalities in health, and this is one of the central themes in the country's health care agreements.

The survey also makes it possible to compare the results across municipalities and regions in Denmark. The results are used by the regions to help the municipalities to ensure that health services and prevention efforts match the local needs of the citizens. The data indicate that populations in rural areas engage in risk-taking behaviour to a larger extent, and have higher morbidity. For example, rates of obesity are highest on the remote island of Læsø (22.6%) and lowest in the Greater Copenhagen area (7.3%). The proportion of people smoking daily is highest on the remote island of Langeland (24.8%), and lowest in the Greater Copenhagen area (8.5%).

The story is the same when it comes to chronic disease burden across the country. The proportion of people with at least one chronic disease by local area ranges from 29.4% to 41%, with the highest rates in more remote areas and the lowest rates in areas closest to the capital and the second-largest city of Aarhus. This is discussed more in Section 2.1. It also suggests there is a need to strengthen the health literacy of poorer populations so they can understand the impacts of risk-taking behaviours and are empowered to engage in self-management of chronic disease.

1.3. Structure of the Danish primary care sector

General practitioners (GPs) play a central role in the Danish health care system. This position has been emphasised further by the administrative and hospital sector reforms of the recent decade. Nevertheless, the organisational structure of the GP sector has not always undergone the necessary changes, notably with regard to co-ordination of services with community care providers, payment methods, and information infrastructure underpinning quality development, to match the increased expectations placed on it.

Major actors, governance and regulation

The primary care sector in Denmark has three political and administrative levels: the state, the five regions and 98 municipalities. This structure was established by the administrative reform of 2007. The task of the state is to formulate overall national health policy and legislation as well as co-ordinate and advise at a general level. Each of the five regions are run by elected councils and are responsible for provision of hospital care, services of office-based specialists, and parts of primary care, including services of general practitioners (GPs), physiotherapy, and dental services for adults. The 98 municipalities are local administrative bodies responsible for home nursing, care homes for elderly, rehabilitation, general disease prevention, and child dental care.

The regional health care services are financed through a block grant and an activity-related subsidy from the state (80%), plus a municipal contribution (20%) consisting of activity-based payments related to use of hospitals. The purpose of the municipal co-payment for hospital services is to encourage the municipality to invest in preventive measures. The municipalities levy local taxes and are additionally supported by lump sum transfers from state.

Nearly all Danish GPs are self-employed professionals working on a contractual basis with the regional authorities. Danish GPs are represented by Organisation of General Practitioners (PLO), whose main function is to conduct collective negotiations of the conditions for provision of GP services with Danish regions – an organisation representing all five regions.

The negotiations between PLO and the regional board of wages and fees (RLTN) are scheduled to take place every three years and establish binding agreements on where, how, and what services are provided by GPs along with the corresponding remuneration. The Health Act and the agreements between PLO and RLTN, form a national regulatory base for the provision of GP services.

Despite the fact that GPs are private sector entities, the provision of their services is subject to far-reaching regulation with regard to permitted number of practices, their geographical distribution, remuneration, number of patients listed with a given practice, and conditions under which patients are accepted by the practice. The system of patient lists is a central characteristic of the system. The regulations set a limit of 1 600 patients per GP, above which a GP can decide to close the list.

The conditions for the provision of community care such as long-term care or rehabilitation, for which the responsibility lies with the municipalities, are defined in a separate round of negotiations between Danish regions and Local Government Denmark (KL) – a national organisation representing all municipalities – without involvement of PLO.

As of 2011, local primary care needs can also be addressed in additional contracts, for services not covered by the national agreement between RLTN and PLO. Further reforms in 2014 encouraged even greater focus on local agreements by taking out conditions for home visits, for example, from nationally-led negotiations. In theory, agreements can be reached between regional collectives of GPs (PLO-R) and individual regions, KL or single municipalities. Negotiations between a collective of GPs in a given municipality (PLO-K) and the local authorities are also permitted, but are not binding. In practice, though, local agreements are rarely, if ever, reached. The PLO advises their members not to negotiate at a local level and rely instead on the regional (PLO-R) or national (PLO).

The 2011 agreement between PLO and Danish regions also created municipal medical committees (KLU), bringing together representatives of local GPs and authorities in each municipality. The primary task of KLU is to discuss issues around co-operation between GPs and community care providers as well as ensure co-ordination of care within the primary sector. KLU can formulate proposals to be included in national negotiations of health agreements but do not have a mandate to implement or take any binding decisions.

In general, the decentralised structure serves the purpose of providing services close to end users well, but may also result in fragmentation of functions. The separation of negotiations between the main actors in the primary sector (most notably, lack of involvement of GPs in the decision making about provision of community care) precludes agreements that facilitate appropriate co-ordination of care within the sector. Similarly, the top-down approach of PLO to agreements is likely to obstruct co-operation at local level within the primary care sector.

GPs' role within the broader health system

Danish GPs act as the first point of contact within the health care system and are responsible for providing longitudinal, on-going management including acute, chronic and preventive health care. Uniquely, GPs are also responsible for integrating physical, psychological, social, cultural and existential dimensions relevant to the patient and her health care concerns.

GPs act also as gatekeepers for non-emergency access to hospital care and services of most of the office-based specialists (except for ophthalmologists and ear, nose and throat specialists) as well as specialist community care and auxiliary services such as physiotherapy. The gatekeeping role makes the GP a central figure in the Danish health care system ensuring that patients are treated at the lowest effective care level – only around 10% of consultations lead to referral specialist health care providers (Pedersen et al., 2012). This closely resembles the models of primary health care in the Netherlands, the United Kingdom as well as other Nordic countries.

There are around 3 500 GPs, distributed across some 2 100practices, currently in practice in Denmark (SSI, 2015). GPs constitute 19% of all physicians, relatively few compared to the OECD average of 29%, but comparable to Scandinavian peers. The GPs' age structure, however, needs to be taken into consideration. In 2015, 30% of all GPs were at least 60 years old and almost 60% at least 50 years old. In nearly 10% of municipalities, more than 50% of GPs were older than 60 years. Moreover, municipalities with a large share of GPs nearing retirement age are also those where the lists of patients are above the limit of 1 600 patients per doctor (KL, 2015). Adjustments to the number medical graduates training in general practice, however, are expected to address any future shortfall in the primary care workforce.

OECD analysis of data on population density, health status, regularity in contacts to GPs, and size of GPs' lists illustrates that there exist geographical disparities in distributions of GPs and their potential workload, as approximated by the size of the patient lists and the population health status. In sparsely populated municipalities, two extremes are observed: GPs with less than 1 100 patients on their list (mostly islands); and GPs with more than 1 700 patients. In densely populated areas most GPs have reached the list size above which they do not have to accept new patients. Moreover, data reveals that there are notable differences in frequency of patient contacts with GPs, which are inversely correlated with health status – the healthiest Danes see their GPs more often than the less healthy part of the population. For detailed discussion of this findings see Section 2.3.

GPs are key actors in the Danish health system and this role should be further strengthened

GPs are key actors in Danish health care system but their co-ordinating role needs to be strengthened, in particular at the interface with the community care providers. For example, it is expected that community nurses can reach any of their patients' GPs via phone or e-mail, or that GPs visit their patients in care homes whenever necessary. This arrangement, however, may be unsustainable given the increasing numbers of frail elderly and earlier hospital discharges. Creation of municipal medical committees (KLU) may fail to resolve these challenges, given the PLO's insistence on nationally-led agreements without local variation.

The allocation of the responsibilities for primary care to two different administrative levels creates a challenge with regard to ensuring appropriate co-ordination of care within the primary sector. Addressing this challenge became particularly important in the view of the recent reconfiguration of the hospital sector, which translates into shorter hospital stays and earlier discharge to community facilities. In other words, a part of the health care services traditionally delivered within the hospital setting is now delivered by the community care providers, which need to work closely with GPs.

Some co-ordination efforts have been made with success but regard the primary and secondary care interface but rarely extend beyond the exchange of patient data. Systematic co-ordination involving all levels of care does not appear to be fully established. Although the possibility for developing the traditional model of primary care through additional local agreements exists, there are only a few examples of local initiatives. For instance, local government in Aarhus (Region Central Jutland) developed home care options for frail elderly and chronic patients by establishing a shared acute unit, which integrates services of GPs and other primary care providers. A similar attempt to improve co-ordination within primary care sector was made in Odense (Region Southern Denmark) between 2013 and 2016, but the initiative was discontinued. In Region Zealand, two municipalities have undertaken efforts to integrate services of GPs, other primary care providers as well as office-based specialists in the so-called *Sundhedshuse* (or "Health Houses"). Evaluation of *Sundhedshuse* reveals, however, that although they offer a various services under one roof, they do not in practice facilitate increased integration of care. More needs to be done, therefore, on the interface between regional and local governments, as well as local primary care providers (KORA, 2016). Without such effort, poor care co-ordination will likely contribute to shortcomings in care, especially for frail elderly populations and individuals with multiple morbidities.

The recent national action plan targeting care for vulnerable elderly patients recognises that little is known about what actions regions and municipalities should implement in order to enhance co-ordination of care for these patients. The action plan allocates DKK 85 million (EUR 11.4 million for the period 2016-19) to development of clinical guidelines in the area of care for elderly and projects investigating possibilities to enhance co-ordination of care. Remarkably, the participation of the GP sector is, however, only mentioned as optional (Sundhedsstyrelsen, 2016; *Aftale om satspuljen på sundheds- og ældreområdet* for 2016-2019, October 2015). Such opportunities should be better exploited, through better involvement of GPs, for Denmark to catch up with countries, where care co-ordination initiatives are already in place.

Several other OECD countries have embarked on detailed and comprehensive plans to deliver better co-ordinated care. The co-ordination reform in Norway is a good example (OECD, 2014a). The Reform introduced substantial economic and organisational changes within the health care system, including establishment of supplemented primary health care units (called *Distriktsmedisinsk senter* or *Sykestue* in Norwegian). These are expected to play a key role in taking care of patients upon discharge from hospital, or where there is a risk of admission to hospitals when the condition could be appropriately managed at a lower intensity care setting. These units are service models for integrated care, financed jointly by hospitals and municipalities.

Another interesting model of Integrated Care Pathways, designed to address chronic diseases, has been adopted in Portugal in 2013. This model takes into account, amongst other dimensions, stratification of risk populations and identification of patients with chronic disease as well as actively involves patients in disease management. The pathways demand the commitment and effective co-ordination of clinical, medical and nursing care delivered by hospitals, primary health care and long term care units. The use of case managers and constitution of multidisciplinary teams facilitates the co-ordination (OECD, 2015b).

In light of the need for better co-ordination in Denmark, the recent agreement between the state, PLO, KL, and Danish regions is particularly welcome (May 2016). Amongst other things, the agreement established a possibility for patients residing at care homes to choose an on-site GP as their regular family doctor. The main rationale behind this change is to improve care quality and in consequence reduce hospital admissions (*Aftale om satspuljen på sundheds og ældreområdet* for 2016-19). Given that a survey of community care homes published in March 2016 found that 90% of care homes do not have a dedicated GP acting as a co-ordinator of care for their residents, this initiative has great potential to improve primary care for individuals with particularly complex needs (Ministry of Social Affairs and Interior, 2016).

Information systems underpinning the delivery, monitoring and evaluation of primary care

Denmark has been a pioneer in the use of clinical quality registers, such as the former Danish General Practice Database (DAMD), which monitored patterns of need, care and some clinical outcomes in primary care. More recent innovation includes the National Health Record (NHR), launched in 2013. The NHR is global electronic patient journal which, until recently, linked data from hospital records, GP records, laboratory results, and cross-sectorial data on medication history via unique patient identifiers. The NHR is accessible by citizens as well as health professionals, excluding community care providers. Patients can also see when and which health professional accesses their data and can choose which data is shared with whom.

In addition, the *Mine diabetesdata* initiative, until recently, allowed patients with diabetes to access cross-sectorial information on their treatment history, including detailed information on medication and test results. It also helped patients understand the data with support of decision aids and other educational material. The aim of *Mine diabetesdata* was to support implementation of the National Board of Health's process programmes for citizens with chronic disease, in particular promoting self-management among patients with diabetes.

In September 2014, however, sharing of data from GP records with the patients as well as health professionals through NHR was terminated due to legal obstacles. Sharing of data from GP records was facilitated through DAMD, which initially collected quality indicators for selected chronic diseases and evolved into general database covering all conditions treated at the primary care level. Upon re-investigation of the legal basis for collection of data in DAMD, the database was deemed not to meet anymore the legal definition for clinical databases, which limits them to disease-specific registers as described in the Assessment and Recommendations section.

The discussion over legality of DAMD register coincided with the 2014 round of negotiations on new health agreement between the two parties, during which PLO strongly opposed ideas of sharing data on DAMD quality indicators at individual practice level with the authorities, fearing that it could be used for monitoring or payment purposes. Eventually, DAMD database was deleted except for few disease specific indicators concerning diabetes, COPD, heart failure and depression in a limited timespan (DAK-E, 2014). The data collection and sharing has not been restored yet.

The above developments not only left the Danish primary care sector with little insight into its performance but also deprived the National Health Record of much of its substance. For example, patients can no longer access information on treatment they received or test results analysed in GP practice. Furthermore, *Mine diabetesdata* was rendered useless, as most of its inputs were extracted from GP journals. The latter is a particularly untoward change for diabetes patients.

The lack of data on primary care performance, especially as compared to other health care sectors, makes it difficult to know how effectively GPs and other primary care professionals are meeting population health care needs. Diseases that are contributing to Danish inequality in health are increasingly treated in primary care. A better data infrastructure would leave Danish authorities better equipped to assure health equity. Unique patient identifiers across health and social care and civil administration databases provide an incredibly rich source of information, rare amongst OECD health systems. These should be marshaled to better monitor health care equity across population groups. It would allow for tools such as cluster-reporting which jointly looks at the contribution from hospitals, GPs and municipalities in individual patients' management. Box 1.1 summarises examples of how primary care data is used in other OECD countries.

There are promising signs of a return to a more data driven system. The recent announcement by PLO (19 May 2016) expressing that GPs are ready, in principle, to resume collection of data on quality indicators and share it with the authorities is an important step. Exactly how the data collection will be executed and under which conditions data will be shared with authorities or made public, however, remains unclear. In particular, whether performance data that allows identification of individual practices will be released has not been clarified.

The parties involved should make all efforts to ensure constructive dialogue and complete the process in the near future. Data on two quality indicators for community care (rehabilitation) is already collected as described in Section 2.3, and publicly shared and development of additional quality indicators is in progress. Work underway to improve the infrastructure for monitoring equality in primary care should continue with most efforts addressing data gaps in GP sector.

Box 1.1 provides illustrations of use of primary care data in other OECD health systems.

Box 1.1. Examples of use of primary care data in OECD countries

Many OECD countries are currently striving to improve primary care, in particular through development and monitoring of evidence-based clinical quality indicators and patient reported outcome measures, as well as public reporting of such indicators (e.g. Norway, Sweden, Italy). Using the indicators for payment is increasingly seen as part of the means to move towards better reimbursement of primary care services, in which quality (including GPs' time spent with a patient) plays a more prominent role (OECD, 2016).

The United Kingdom has become a point of reference in this field. The UK's *Quality and Outcomes Framework*, system-wide measurement of activities and outcomes achieved within primary care, is an internationally known scheme to improve processes and outcomes in general practice. It was one of the earliest international schemes to link quality indicators to pay-for-performance (P4P) scheme, at system-wide level. From its inception, the framework was detailed and ambitious, and it now covers a range of clinical areas, with focus on long-term conditions and associated risk factors. For example, target outcomes were specified for particular clinical groups, such as achieving blood pressures of 145/85 or less in at least 85% of diabetics. The framework is continuously evolving and its design has been adapted to local contexts in each of the four health systems of the United Kingdom (OECD, 2016).

Alongside the *Quality and Outcomes Framework* in the United Kingdom, Israel has developed another rich programme for monitoring the quality of primary care among OECD countries. Over the past decade and a half, policy makers and health plans have sought to reorganise doctors working in the community into teams. This has provided them with a platform to do things that other OECD countries are struggling to do, like regular monitoring of a patient's health indicators, delivering follow-up support after a visit to the GP, and tailoring preventative advice to the specific needs of communities. These efforts are often supported by information technology platforms such as those that remind clinic staff which patients have not received a regular check-up.

Box 1.1. Examples of use of primary care data in OECD countries *(cont.)*

A major strength of primary care in Israel is the extensive range of data that is collected by community health facilities on nearly the entire population. The basis for this has been electronic patient records that have facilitated the collection of information on patients, and has led to the specification of a minimum data set called the *Quality Indicators in Community Health Care* (QICH) programme. The QICH includes basic patient demographics and 35 measures across six key areas: asthma, cancer screening, and immunisation for the elderly, children's health, cardiovascular health and diabetes. This data identify some risk factors for poor health (*e.g.* obesity), monitor the quality of care being delivered, track drug utilisation and measure selected treatment outcomes (OECD, 2012).

Payment system underpinning the delivery of primary care

GPs are paid through a mixed system comprising both capitation sums (about 30% of GP income) and fee-for-service sums (about 70%), negotiated between PLO and Danish regions. Fees are earned on consultations, home visits and minor surgery; some preventive health care work also attracts a fee, such as preventive dialogues with patients, vaccinations or child health programmes.

There is, however, no direct quality-related component in the current payment structure. A limited pay-for-performance scheme linked to quality indicators based on outcomes in treatment of diabetes was added in 2007, in which GPs could participate on voluntary basis. The scheme was, however, discontinued in 2014 due to low uptake and the collapse of DAMD database. In consequence, the preventive work with diabetes patients is again reimbursed with the general fee for any kind of a preventive dialogue sessions with patients.

The payment system for GP services has remained largely unchanged during last decade with regard to both, the level of (inflation-adjusted) payment and the itemised services. This means that the payment system does not correspond well with the challenges brought about by the recent reforms rebalancing care away from the hospital to the primary sector. Nor does it reflect the potential workload related to the growing share of elderly population and burden of chronic diseases.

A growing number of OECD countries modernise GP remuneration systems with elements of pay-for-performance (P4P) or re-definition of services such that they cover entire (often long-term) episodes of care. P4P based on quality indicators has been shown to reduce unwarranted variation in care, particularly for chronic conditions and has been associated with fewer hospital admissions. For example, targeted incentives on the compliance to clinical practice guidelines had favourable effects on diabetes outcomes in the United Kingdom (OECD, 2016b).

In Japan, a modernised fee schedule serves as a major policy lever. The fees not only reward quantity but also incentivise quality by specifying minimum inputs, and in some cases indicators linked to outcomes. The schedule includes also new items such as a fee rewarding for the setting up co-ordinated community care plans upon a patient's discharge.

References

Christensen, M.B., M. Gortz and M. Kallestrup-Lamb (2016), "Medical Spending in Denmark", *Fiscal Studies*, Vol. 37, No. 3-4, pp. 461-497.

Dalton, S.O. et al. (2008), "Social Inequality in Incidence of and Survival from Cancer in a Population-based Study in Denmark, 1994–2003: Summary of Findings", *European Journal of Cancer*, Vol. 44, No. 2008, pp. 2074-2085.

KL – Local Government Denmark (2015), *Analyse: Kortlægning af lægedækningen i Danmark*, September.

KORA – Det Nationale Institut for Kommuners og Regioners Analyse og Forskning, (2016), *Status og fremadrettede perspektiver for udvikling og samarbajde: Nakskov Sundhedscenter og Kalundborg Sundheds- og Akuthus samt Lægecenter*, Copenhagen.

Ministry of Social Affairs and Interior (2016), "Ankestyrelsens kortlægning af Plejeboligområdet", Denmark, March.

OECD (2016a), *Better Ways to Pay for Health Care*, OECD Publishing, Paris, http://dx.doi.org/10.1787/9789264258211-en.

OECD (2016b), *OECD Reviews of Health Care Quality: United Kingdom 2016: Raising Standards*, OECD Publishing, Paris, http://dx.doi.org/10.1787/9789264239487-en.

OECD (2015a), *In It Together: Why Less Inequality Benefits All*, OECD Publishing, Paris, http://dx.doi.org/10.1787/9789264235120-en.

OECD (2015b), *OECD Reviews of Health Care Quality: Portugal 2015: Raising Standards*, OECD Publishing, Paris, http://dx.doi.org/10.1787/9789264225985-en.

OECD (2014a), *OECD Reviews of Health Care Quality: Norway 2014: Raising Standards*, OECD Publishing, Paris, http://dx.doi.org/10.1787/9789264208469-en.

OECD (2012), *OECD Reviews of Health Care Quality: Israel 2012: Raising Standards*, OECD Publishing, Paris, http://dx.doi.org/10.1787/9789264029941-en.

Pedersen, K.M. et al. (2012), "General Practice and Primary Health Care in Denmark", *Journal of American Board of Family Medicine*, Vol. 25, Suppl. 1, pp. S34-S38, http://dx.doi.org/10.3122/jabfm.2012.02.110216.

Sundhedsstyrelsen (2016), *Styrket indsats for den ældre medicinske patient Fagligt oplæg til en handlingsplan 2016-2019*, April.

SSI (2015), *Synlighed om resultater i sundhedsvæsenet*, February.

Ullits, L.R. et al. (2015), "Socioeconomic Inequality and Mortality – A Regional Danish Cohort Study", *BMC Public Health*, Vol. 15:490, http://dx.doi.org/10.1186/s12889-015-1813-3.

World Bank (2016), "Urban Population (% of total)", available at: http://data.worldbank.org/indicator/SP.URB.TOTL.IN.ZS (accessed 04/05/2016).

Database references

OECD Health Statistics 2016, http://dx.doi.org/10.1787/health-data-en.

OECD Historical Population Data and Projections Database, 2015, https://data.oecd.org/pop/population.htm.

OECD Income Distribution Database (IDD), http://www.oecd.org/social/income-distribution-database.htm.

Chapter 2

The performance of Danish primary care

While Danish GPs have fulfilled the primary care function very well over many years, the challenges outline above demand a different, stronger and modernised primary care sector. This has not yet convincingly emerged. Health system reforms in recent years have focused on efforts to improve quality and efficiency in the hospital sector – relegating modernisation of the primary care sector to a more cautious and incremental path.

The statistical data for Israel are supplied by and under the responsibility of the relevant Israeli authorities. The use of such data by the OECD is without prejudice to the status of the Golan Heights, East Jerusalem and Israeli settlements in the West Bank under the terms of international law.

2.1. The accessibility of primary care

Reforms in the organisation of out-of-hours primary care have reduced the workload for Danish GPs without compromising patient satisfaction

The provision of out-of-hours (OOH) care has been a challenging issue for many OECD countries. Much of this is due to the burden for GPs of working many late nights, particularly in more isolated areas where fewer doctors means a greater workload. The standard day-time opening hours for Danish GPs are 8am to 4pm Monday to Friday. This is a slightly shorter day compared to some other countries. For example, the standard day-time hours for Dutch GPs is 8am to 5pm. In England, GPs are expected to make routine appointments available between 8am and 6.30pm on weekdays (NHS, 2016).

The dominant model of OOH primary care in Denmark is the general practice co-operative (GPC). These are large-scale co-operatives in which self-organising GPs work together on a rotational basis to respond to the OOH care needs for all the patients in a particular area. According to the agreement between the regions and the PLO, GPs are collectively obliged to participate in OOH primary care, but exemptions may apply due to circumstances such as age. Exemptions can also apply if some GPs wish to do more of the OOH workload to earn a higher income, relieving other GPs of OOH participation. GPs are given a financial incentive to participate in the form of higher fees for OOH services (it is free for patients). Patients call a single telephone number in a region to determine whether they need to attend the clinic, need a home visit or can be managed on the telephone. In more serious cases, patients may be advised to go to a hospital emergency department. Telephone triage is performed by GPs. The exception is in the Capital Region of Copenhagen, where telephone triage is performed by nurses (Berchet and Nader, 2016).

Denmark was an early adopter of the GPC model in 1992, and other countries such as the Netherlands have adopted similar models. The Danish changes came about largely due to GPs' dissatisfaction with the OOH workload. Before the changes, OOH care was provided by patients' own GPs, and later several GPs in an area joined a rota system to run an OOH service at a smaller scale to the current GPCs. A 1998 evaluation showed the reform had a rapid impact on doctors' workload. Home visits declined from 46% to 18%, telephone consultations almost doubled to 48%, and face-to-face consultations rose from 24% to 33%.

The total number of OOH services decreased by 11% just after the reform, but then reached a level 1% higher than before the reform. Patient satisfaction declined slightly after the reform, but then began rising again (Christensen and Olesen, 1998). A 2009 national survey showed that nearly 80% of patients were satisfied with OOH primary care service and only 11% were dissatisfied due to experiencing either excessive waiting times or problems with communication (Sundhedsstyrelsen, 2009).

Chronic disease is strongly associated with the use of OOH primary care services in Denmark. A study of almost 14 000 patients, conducted in the OOH service of the Central Denmark Region, found almost 5 000 patients had at least one of five nominated chronic diseases: chronic lung disease, heart disease, diabetes, psychiatric disease, and cancer. Patients with chronic disease were more often managed by OOH GPs than patients who did not have chronic conditions (Flarup et al., 2014).

When compared with the Dutch OOH system, the Danish population relies upon the OOH system to a greater extent. In a two-month period, there were 80 OOH care contacts per 1 000 population in Denmark, compared with 50 per 1 000 in the Netherlands. The Danish population had more telephone consultations and home visits, while the Dutch had more clinic consultations. The biggest difference was in the youngest patients. The study is confirmed in national statistics indicating that Danish consumption of OOH care is about double that of Dutch consumption (Huibers et al., 2014). It is possible that one explanatory factor for these differences is the OOH period begins one hour earlier in Denmark than it does in the Netherlands. However, this is likely to explain only some of the difference. Another possible factor could be that calling the telephone triage line gets Danish patients direct access to a GP, whereas in the Netherlands it is nurses who perform the triage under the supervision of GPs. Perhaps, therefore, patients in Denmark are more likely to seek telephone medical advice as it is an easy way for them to talk to a GP.

Unlike the Danish model, however, the model in the Netherlands integrates the GPC with hospital emergency departments in some regions. Patients are triaged at one point, and directed either to the GPC or the emergency department. Under this system, patients cannot self-refer to the emergency department. Several studies in the Netherlands found the integrated model has the potential to reduce health system costs, as it is associated with a reduction in patient self-referrals to the emergency department (Berchet and Nader, 2016).

It is surprising that Denmark still relies on GPs to perform telephone triage when many other countries use nurses to perform this function. This is likely to be in part to resistance from the doctors' lobby. Such resistance was clearly manifest by the PLO's advice to members to boycott the OOH model in the Capital Region, because of nurses' participation in telephone triage (PLO, 2013), even though it was designed to increase choice and access for patients.

Yet a survey of more than 1 000 Danish citizens who used the Copenhagen OOH telephone line in 2015 indicates satisfaction is high. Of those who called, 39% spoke only with a nurse, and 33% spoke with a nurse first, then a physician. In some cases GPs answer the phone, and 28% spoke only with a GP. The service's potential to reduce the use of more costly health services is clear. Almost half (48%) of those who called were helped on the telephone, while 52% were referred further in the health system (Region Hovedstaden – Enhed for Evaluering og Brugerinddragelse, 2015). The survey also suggests there is little difference in the experience patients had with nurses and doctors (Figure 2.1). Patients reported high satisfaction with both professions.

However, the survey indicates that waiting times for the service are more of an issue (Figure 2.2). Some 43% of people reported the waiting time for contact was too long, while 37% reported the time to be put through to a doctor was too long. This suggests a need to expand the availability of doctors for those patients (just over half) whose cases were not resolved by nurses. If the PLO were to drop its boycott of the service, this would presumably be a significant step toward develop this capacity and improving patient satisfaction.

Box 2.1. Telephone triage in primary care

A large body of literature has examined the safety of telephone triage. Much of the literature indicates it is safe when used with computerised decision support and accompanied by appropriate training for health professionals (Berchet and Nader, 2016). Lattimer et al. (1998) and Dale et al. (2004) are among those who found nurse telephone triage supported by decision support software, such as computerised clinical decision support, was safe and effective. In addition, Lattimer et al. (1998) concluded nurse telephone consultation reduced the overall workload of GPs by 50%, while allowing callers faster access to information.

In Australia, an audit of the Nurse-on-Call telephone line concluded it was overall safe and cost-effective, although there was scope to improve the quality of advice given. Total reported incidents were extremely low at 105 out of 1.47 million calls, although 4% of calls reviewed through mystery caller testing did not meet clinical safety standards (Victorian Auditor-General, 2010). In Norway, where local emergency medical communication centres are usually staffed with registered nurses, a study found the mean of total correct responses among the nurses was 78%, ranging from 45% to 95%. In total, 12% of all assessments were under-triaged, and 18% were over-triaged. The authors concluded that the quality of nurse decision making was high (Hansen and Hunskaar, 2011). However, a systematic review found that on average, about 10% of telephone triage contacts were unsafe. Studies that used simulated high-risk patients showed that on average about 50% were unsafe. The types of adverse events reported included mortality, unplanned hospitalisations, unplanned ED attendance, and medical errors (Huibers et al., 2011). No comparison with GP-led telephone triage was made.

In the Netherlands, a cross-sectional study found the appropriate triage outcome was reached in 58% of calls. Urgency was under-estimated in 41% of calls, and over-estimated in 1% (Derkx et al., 2008). Another study in the Netherlands indicated telephone triage nurses under-estimated the level of urgency of 19% of contacts. There was a significant correlation between the accurate estimation of the urgency and specific training on telephone guidelines, indicating training can help improve safety of care. However, the study was not designed to compare nurse triage with GP-led triage, and the authors noted perhaps the telephone itself was an unsafe medium (Giesen et al., 2007). Concerns can also arise over the quality of telephone triage delivered by doctors.

In Italy, a cross-sectional study showed that the quality of telephone triage by doctors, in terms of mandatory questions asked during simulated calls, was low. The proportion of obligatory questions asked compared with those expected to be asked was 36% in the clinical case of a child with vomiting; 32% in the case of a child with fever; 28% in the case of an adult with fever; and 27% for an adult with nosebleed. However, the ability to assess the case, the clinical management decisions made and the treatment advised was almost always appropriate (Pasini et al., 2015). Overall, a Cochrane systematic review of nine studies found telephone consultations appeared to be as safe as face-to-face consultations. There was no evidence of an increase in adverse effects (Bunn et al., 2004).

Figure 2.1. Patient satisfaction with the Copenhagen out-of-hours telephone triage service

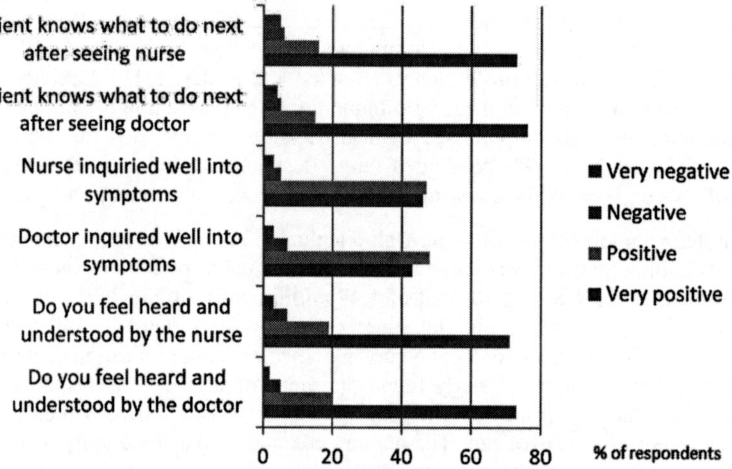

Source: Adapted from: Region Hovedstade – Enhed for Evaluering og Brugerinddragelse (2015), "Borgernes oplevelser af Akuttelefonen 1813: Telefonsurvey blandt 1.106 borgere, der har ringet til 1813", revised edition, 30 April 2015.

Figure 2.2. Satisfaction with waiting times at the Copenhagen out-of-hours telephone triage service

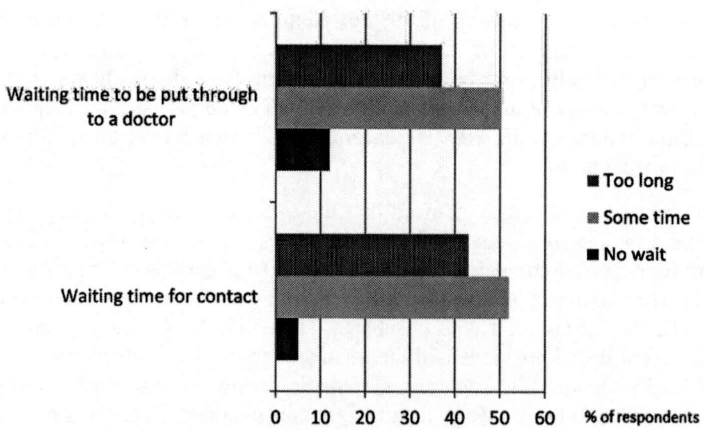

Source: Adapted from: Region Hovedstade – Enhed for Evaluering og Brugerinddragelse (2015), "Borgernes oplevelser af Akuttelefonen 1813: Telefonsurvey blandt 1.106 borgere, der har ringet til 1813", revised edition, 30 April 2015.

A large body of literature has examined the safety of telephone triage, and there is little evidence to suggest it is associated with a higher risk of adverse events when conducted by nurses. Much of the literature indicates it is safe when used with computerised decision support and accompanied by appropriate training for health professionals (Berchet and Nader, 2016). Lattimer et al. (1998) and Dale et al. (2004) are among those who found nurse telephone triage supported by decision support software, such as computerised clinical decision support, was safe and effective. In addition, Lattimer et al. (1998) concluded nurse telephone consultation reduced the overall workload of GPs by 50%, while allowing callers faster access to information.

Denmark should therefore explore the feasibility of moving towards a nurse-led telephone-triage system in OOH services. This could be done under the supervision of GPs, as with the Netherlands model. A pilot of this model outside the Copenhagen Region should be considered as part of the 2017 health agreement. To alleviate concerns about the impact on patient safety, a randomised controlled trial should be conducted, comparing nurse telephone triage and GP telephone triage, and the impact on patient outcomes. If findings are positive, Denmark should consider implementing this model across the country. Denmark could also consider piloting the integration of the out-of-hours primary care centre with the hospital emergency department, starting with a small-scale pilot and rolling out the model if it is proven to be effective in reducing self-referrals to emergency departments, without compromising on patient safety and satisfaction.

Use of primary care services in Denmark's more remote areas is inversely related to need

According to the Danish Health Act, it is a regional responsibility to provide basic medical coverage in primary care. This responsibility is implemented through a collective agreement with the Danish GPs Medical Association (PLO), which is negotiated every three years. The agreement also stipulates that all patients should be able to choose between two GP clinics within 15 kilometres from their home. However, there are cases where it is difficult to meet this requirement.

Denmark is a small country, but as with many OECD countries, nevertheless faces challenges in ensuring good access to health care services in its more remote areas. Some of the more remote islands, for example, have small populations. Primary care arrangements are decided locally, depending on the distance to the coast, population and the possibility of recruiting GPs to live on the islands. Larger islands have their own GPs. If islands are close to the mainland, they can visit GPs in nearby cities. However, island populations that are very small and remote are often attended by an island nurse, supported by an acute response capability and phone service when needed.

Data from Danish National Health Profile indicates that communities in remote areas contact their primary care provider least regularly - less often than once per year – despite the fact that the self-rated health is worst in these areas and that list sizes are typically smaller than in cities (see Figure 2.18). This suggests a complex relationship between use of primary care services and health, inversely related to need. Possible explanations include lower levels of health literacy in more rural areas, or problems with access due to longer travel times to a GP practice, compared to more densely populated areas.

Remote regions can use a range of measures defined in the agreement and the Health Act to deal with these challenges. For instance, changes to the Health Act in 2013 made it possible for regions to outsource general medicine services to a private health care provider that employs GPs outside the terms of the agreement, or establish an intermediate regional primary health care clinic. A national committee is currently considering other options to improve access. Options being considered include giving the regions more leverage on where GPs are located; making general practice in remote areas more appealing to younger GPs through incentives; and initiatives that support older GPs to delay retirement through more flexible working, such as having the option of seeing fewer patients.

Greater flexibility in use of the health care workforce should be extended to primary care

With chronic disease anticipated to grow in Denmark, there is a need to rethink how health care services are provided. One way Denmark can do this is by boosting the role that nurses play in primary care. For example, the primary care systems in Sweden and Finland feature multidisciplinary health centres with nurses as the first point of contact, referring patients to GPs or hospital if necessary. This expanded role for nurses was in part driven by a shortage of GPs in these countries. Sweden has taken the expansion of nurses' tasks further by authorising some nurses to prescribe drugs in limited circumstances (Bourgueil et al., 2005). This is still a practice widely considered controversial in many countries. However, an evaluation in England found that overall, both nurse and pharmacist prescribing is safe and clinically appropriate, and patient satisfaction is high (Latter et al., 2010). Nurses can safely perform this function in specified circumstances, and when they have the appropriate qualifications and training.

Nurse practitioners do not exist in Denmark, in contrast to many other comparable countries. For example, nurse practitioners are reasonably well-established in primary care in Sweden. Their functions include independently taking care of conditions such as upper pulmonary infections, urinary tract infections, otitis, dermatitis and skin problems (Lindblad et al., 2010). In another model that Denmark could consider, the United Kingdom has minor injury units led by nurse practitioners. One of the goals of these units is to help avoid unnecessary OOH visits to emergency departments by treating patients who can be appropriately managed in that setting (Berchet and Nader, 2016).

Danish research suggests that there is scope for doctor-nurse substitution. In one study, GPs deemed substitution was possible in 15% of consultations. Patients considered substitution was possible in 12% of consultations. However, GPs and patients agreed on the cases where substitution could take place in just 3.5% of consultations (Nørøxe et al., 2013). Better alignment of perspectives can be achieved by educating both clinicians and patients as to the role that nurses can safely and effectively play.

Using nurses differently should not be too confronting a move in Denmark, as there have been other experiments in the country involving role substitution. For instance, the Association of Medical Specialists (FAPS) and the Danish regions re-evaluate task delegation when they negotiate their agreements, and it is up to specialists to decide if they wish to participate in these trials. As part of the agreement, there is a reduced fee for clinical staff, such as nurses, audiologists and optometrists, to perform certain tasks. In one example, some ophthalmologists permit other clinical staff to perform Optical Coherence Tomography (OCT) scans on patients, and the scans are evaluated by specialists. One trial showed that this could free up specialists to spend time doing more high-level clinical work with other patients. More than 138 000 diabetic patients were able to have every second OCT scan performed by other clinical staff.

In another trial that began in April 2016, gynaecologists can permit clinical staff to consult with patients with regards to incontinence, abortion, changing vaginal ring and examining sperm tests. In another trial due to start in October 2016, clinical staff working in internal medicine will be able to perform functions including administering vaccinations and performing tests such as spirometry.

Nurses play a less prominent role in primary care in Denmark, although the Nurses' Association reports that there is a willingness from the nursing profession to take on more. Nurses could quickly take on a bigger role, for example, in those municipalities which have set up health centres that offer primary care, rehabilitation and other services through multidisciplinary teams. Innovation and leadership from both clinical staff and facility managers will be vital to develop nurses' roles in such settings. There is also a need, however, to change the structure of nursing education. Currently, it is too general to support specialisation in nursing for general practice and primary health care. This transformation should take place not only because nurses wish to take on more, but also because there will be a growing need for them to do so. As Denmark's demography changes, nurses will need to take on more chronic disease management and health promotion activities.

Denmark's innovations in telehealth offer lessons to other OECD primary care systems

Another key way Denmark has been seeking to improve access to health services is through a more co-ordinated use of technology. The country has tried a series of telehealth initiatives that would be of interest to other OECD countries (Box 2.2).

Box 2.2. The use of telehealth in Denmark

Telehealth has the potential to expand access to health services, particularly in rural areas. Such technology links patients to clinicians, or remote GPs to specialists at major hospitals. Denmark is moving towards a more co-ordinated use of telehealth, with the launch of a 2012 National Telemedicine Action Plan. In one initiative, there are plans to nationally implement clinically-integrated home monitoring (Klinisk Integreret Hjemmemonitorering – the KIH project) by the end of 2019. KIH began as a pilot that tested the benefit of telehealth for 2 000 patients with chronic obstructive pulmonary disease (COPD), diabetes, chronic inflammatory intestinal disease, as well as pregnant women. In recognition that these patients require extensive contact with health services and co-ordination between providers, patients use technology installed at home to measure and register relevant data about their own health. A technical hub ensures that all clinicians have access to the data and patient treatment plans via their specialist systems. Clinicians monitor the data and report relevant information back to patients via video consultation. The patients can register data, look up their treatment plans, find relevant information and book appointments. It is hoped that this will be nationally implemented by the end of 2019.

Box 2.2. The use of telehealth in Denmark *(cont.)*

Another telehealth project due to be rolled out nationally is the telemedical wound assessment. A municipal nurse attends to patients' wounds in their own homes by taking photos of the wounds and sending them to a clinician at the hospital as an online health record that can be accessed by both clinicians and the patient. This initiative also aims to reduce hospitalisations and transport time for patients.

Local initiatives also sit within the National Telemedicine Action Plan. One is Telecare North, for patients with COPD. The project involves 11 municipalities and local GPs in North Jutland Region, and Aalborg University. The objective is to monitor patients closely, adjust their medication and treatment, and avoid hospitalisation. Participating patients are given a small bag to take home, containing devices enabling them to measure their oxygen saturation, pulse, blood pressure, and weight twice a week. The measurements are transmitted via a small tablet computer to health care staff in the patient's municipality or at the local hospital. The staff monitor the data and provide further counselling to the patient if necessary. The information empowers patients by helping them to understand what they can do to manage their condition. Insights from Telecare North were instrumental in developing business case and implementation plans for nationwide telecare programmes.

Source: Information supplied by Danish authorities.

2.2. Quality measurement and improvement

Health policy makers are increasingly turning their attention to the quality and value of health services. This is in recognition of the fact that high-quality health care improves patients' outcomes, and also equates to value for money. Between 2012 and 2016, the OECD conducted a series of reviews examining the quality of 15 health systems (including Denmark in 2013). The OECD's assessment of quality of health care encompasses effectiveness, safety and responsiveness. Table 2.1 provides a description of policies that influence health care quality the OECD used as a framework in conducting the health system quality reviews.

Table 2.1. A typology of health care policies that influence health care quality

Policy	Examples
Health system design	Accountability of actors, allocation of responsibilities, legislation
Health system inputs (professionals, organisations, technologies)	Professional licensing, accreditation of health care organisations, quality assurance of drugs and medical devices
Health system monitoring and standardisation of practice	Measurement of quality of care, national standards and guidelines, national audit studies and reports on performance
Improvement (national programmes, hospital programmes and incentives)	National programmes on quality and safety, pay for performance in hospital care, examples of improvement programmes within institutions

General practice needs to play a more substantial role in managing chronic disease

In seeking to promote high quality primary care, particular attention should be given to the sector's ability to respond to the rising number of people with complex, chronic conditions, and avoiding the need for such patients to go to hospital. GPs need to be given the incentive to take on the role of co-ordinating the care of these patients.

Under the current agreement between the PLO and the regions, GPs are intended to play a central role as case managers and gatekeepers to the health system. The agreement stipulates that GPs are expected to care for the population on their list by performing activities such as monitoring certain risk groups, particularly patients with chronic disease.

Changes in 2007 gave responsibility for primary prevention, including the early detection of risk factors such as tobacco and alcohol consumption, to the municipalities. Secondary prevention (e.g. screening) and tertiary prevention (e.g. reducing the consequences once a disease has developed) remain shared responsibilities between the municipalities, regions and GPs. The agreement says GPs should refer suitable patients to municipality prevention services, and obliges GPs to talk about prevention with their patients.

Of note, the list system in Danish general practice means that GPs do not have to compete for patients. Such a system provides little incentive for GPs to do anything extra such as offer longer opening hours, adopt the role of case manager, or to spend time engaging in preventive health activities. Nor does the payment system (discussed earlier) provide this incentive.

Potentially avoidable hospitalisations are an indirect indicator of the extent to which Danish primary care needs to do better to manage chronic conditions to keep people out of hospital. With hospital length of stay a declining trend across the OECD, primary care is also now required to manage patients with chronic conditions earlier, at a time when they are sicker than they were when they were discharged from hospital in the past.

In Denmark, two out of three indicators – potentially avoidable hospitalisations for COPD and diabetes (Figures 2.3 and 2.4) – show a clear downward trend, although the rates in Denmark are still higher than selected comparable countries. Potentially avoidable hospitalisations for asthma, however, increased slightly in Denmark from 41.8 per 100 000 in 2007, to 45.9 per 100 000 population in 2013 (Figure 2.5). Although asthma admission rates remain lower than peer comparators, Sweden's rates suggest there is still room for further improvement in Denmark (OECD Health Statistics, 2016).

Figure 2.3. COPD hospital admissions, age-sex standardised rate per 100 000 population

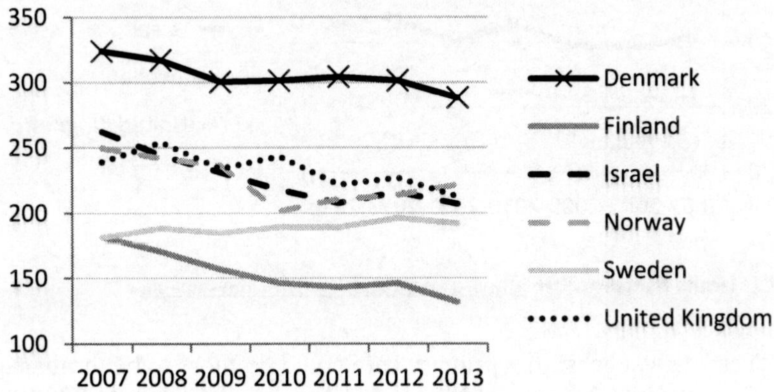

Source: OECD Health Statistics 2016, http://dx.doi.org/10.1787/health-data-en.

Figure 2.4. Diabetes hospital admissions, age-sex standardised rate per 100 000 population

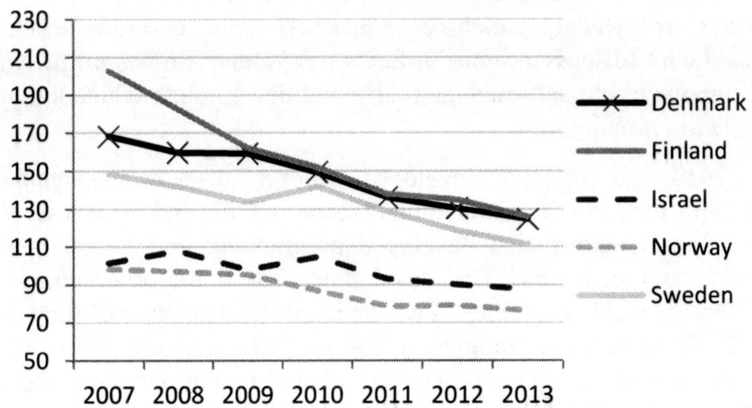

Source: OECD Health Statistics 2016, http://dx.doi.org/10.1787/health-data-en.

Figure 2.5. Asthma hospital admissions, age-sex standardised rate per 100 000 population

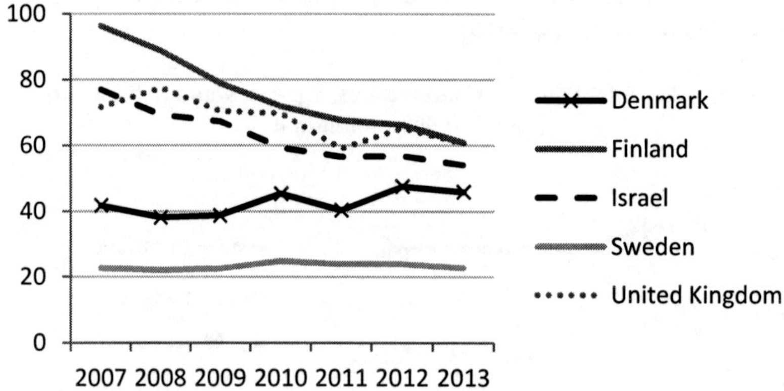

Source: OECD Health Statistics 2016, http://dx.doi.org/10.1787/health-data-en.

These data suggest that primary care could do more to better manage some key chronic diseases and keep people out of hospital. In 2008, the Danish Health Authority, the regions and municipalities developed a generic model for chronic disease management programmes, including one for diabetes. The philosophy was to strengthen the co-ordination between primary and secondary care, as well as municipal services for people with chronic disease. Arrangements are broadly based on the Chronic Care Model, which encompasses more co-ordinated and integrated care (discussed more in Section 2.4), and a focus on patients being empowered to self-manage their condition through education and rehabilitation programmes.

In 2014, all regions developed chronic disease management programmes for conditions including diabetes, COPD and cardiovascular disease. Some regions also developed programmes for mental health conditions and dementia. The development of these programmes is guided by clinical guidelines and national legislation, so they are generally the same across regions. It is too soon to tell what effects these programmes have had thus far, and they should be thoroughly evaluated to inform the future direction of chronic disease management in Denmark.

Denmark's poor cancer survival rates point to delayed diagnosis and, possibly, difficulties in accessing specialist care

Cancer survival rates can be influenced by factors such as good screening programmes targeted at the right populations, and timely diagnosis and treatment. In this regard, Denmark fares poorly compared with other countries. For example, the CONCORD-2 study shows that Denmark's five-year age-standardised net survival rate for adults with colon cancer was 55.9% for the period 2005-09. This is low compared with its Nordic peers of Finland (62.9%), Iceland (65.1%), and Norway (61.8%) and Sweden (62.5%). Similarly, for lung cancer, Denmark's five-year age-standardised net survival for adults was 11.3% for the period 2005-2009, compared with Finland (12.3%), Iceland (15%), Norway (15%) and Sweden (15.6%) (Allemani et al., 2014).

Another study comparing Nordic countries found lower survival for Danish cancer patients in 23 of the 33 cancer sites in men and 26 of 35 sites in women. It concluded that the differences in Nordic cancer patient survival could be linked to national variations in risk factors (see Section 1.2 for Danish indicators on risk factors such as tobacco, alcohol and obesity), co-morbidity, and the implementation of screening (Storm et al., 2010).

OECD data confirm Denmark has a poorer survival record for breast cancer (Figure 2.6) and colorectal cancer (Figure 2.7), compared with other Nordic countries, although the survival rate for each has improved. Denmark fares better when it comes to survival for cervical cancer (Figure 2.8) (OECD Health Statistics, 2016). This may be due to more concerted efforts to educate people about the need for regular cervical screening.

Figure 2.6. Breast cancer five-year relative survival, 1998-2003 and 2008-13 (or nearest periods)

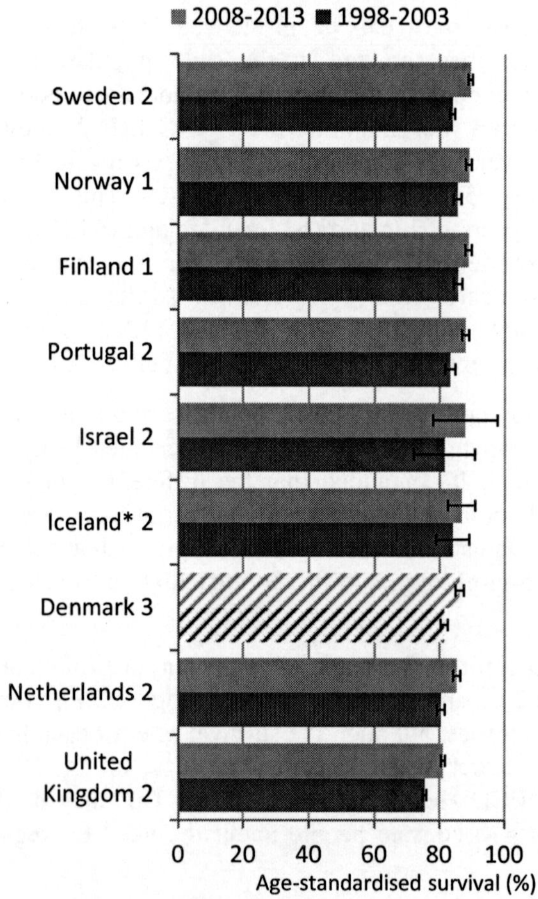

Note: * Three-period average. 95% confidence intervals represented by H.

1. Period analysis.

2. Cohort analysis.

3. Different analysis methods used for different years.

Source: OECD Health Statistics 2016, http://dx.doi.org/10.1787/health-data-en.

Figure 2.7. Colorectal cancer five-year relative survival, 1998-2003 and 2008-13 (or nearest periods)

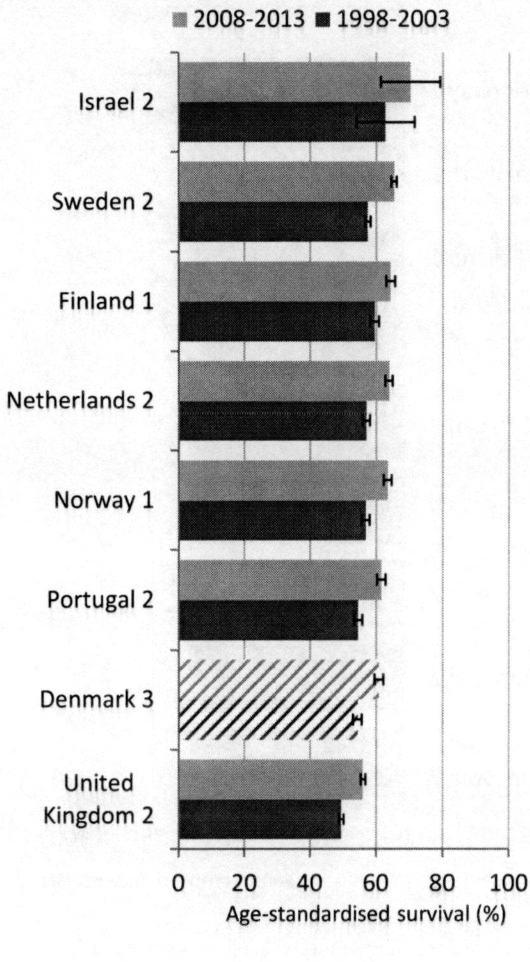

Note: * Three-period average. 95% confidence intervals represented by H.

1. Period analysis.

2. Cohort analysis.

3. Different analysis methods used for different years.

Source: OECD Health Statistics 2016, http://dx.doi.org/10.1787/health-data-en

Figure 2.8. Cervical cancer five-year relative survival, 1998-2003 and 2008-13 (or nearest periods)

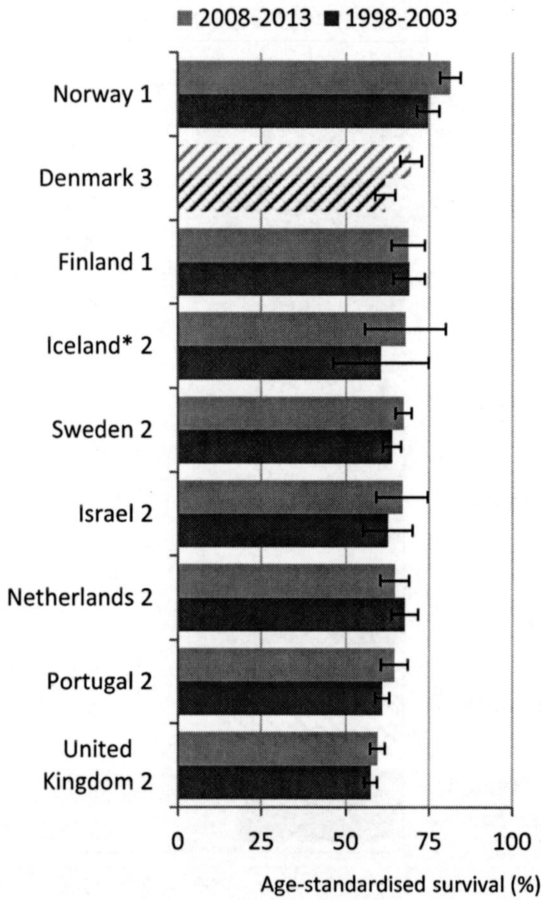

Note: * Three-period average. 95% confidence intervals represented by H.

1. Period analysis.

2. Cohort analysis.

3. Different analysis methods used for different years.

Source: OECD Health Statistics 2016, http://dx.doi.org/10.1787/health-data-en.

Denmark has sought to develop strategies to close the survival gap with its Nordic peers. It developed care pathways (*forløbsbeskrivelser*) for different types of cancer, in 2007. The pathways include clinical guidelines and time standards for different stages, from diagnostics to treatment. There are more than 30 different cancer-specific pathways. In addition, the regions have implemented a diagnostic fast-track pathway for patients with unspecific symptoms of serious disease that could be cancer. A monitoring system for the cancer pathways, based on data from the National Patient Registry and the Cancer Register, is set up and overall cancer trends are being monitored, such as the time from referral to hospital to initiation of treatment.

For a large group of patients, the pathways have improved the time to diagnosis. For example, a lung cancer pathway enables GPs to refer patients they suspect of having lung cancer directly to fast-track diagnostics. In one study, two-thirds of lung cancer patients were seen in general practice before they were diagnosed and a quarter of identified lung cancer patients were diagnosed through the fast-track route. However, there was also a high incidence of patients undergoing multiple x-rays due to problems with the sensitivity of chest x-rays used to diagnose lung cancer. The study concluded that fast-track pathways were insufficient to ensure earlier lung cancer diagnosis (Guldbrandt et al., 2015).

The ordering of multiple tests points to the need to provide GPs with more support and training to help them identify symptoms of cancer, without relying on screening alone. This lack of awareness can lengthen the time to diagnosis, potentially compromising survival. A study identifying GP self-reported "quality deviations" (an event that should not have happened) in the diagnostic pathway in general practice found such quality deviations existed in 30% of cancer patients. The presence of a quality deviation increased the diagnostic interval by a median of 41 days. The most common quality deviation was that GPs considered that retrospectively, one or more of their clinical decisions were less optimal. This was more common among patients with vague symptoms (Jensen et al., 2014).

To address these issues, the government and the regions recently agreed to implement various tools in order to help GP's detecting cancer in earlier stages. Among the tools are fast-track access to diagnostics, easier access to specialist guidance from the hospitals, and education in symptoms of cancer. Moreover, the diagnostic capacity in the hospitals has been increased significantly. Another important effort worth mentioning is the introduction of a national screening programme for colorectal cancer in 2014.

Denmark's national cancer plans in 2000 and 2005 noted the survival deficit compared with Nordic and neighbouring countries (Coleman et al., 2011). Yet more than a decade later, Denmark continues to fare poorly on cancer survival (particularly breast and colorectal cancer) compared with other countries. GPs have the potential to play a more substantial role in the prevention of risk factors, as well as in earlier detection of cancer.

There is also a need to educate and reassure the public, who may be reluctant to see a doctor to assess cancer due to anxiety or a lack of understanding of how GPs can help. For instance, a population-based telephone interview with 3 000 people found concern about what the doctor might find. Concern about wasting the doctor's time was reported by 27% and 15% of respondents, respectively. These were barriers for attending a GP (Hvidberg et al., 2015). As outlined in Section 1.1, social inequalities are also associated with poorer cancer survival. There is a need for interventions designed to strengthen health literacy to reduce risk-taking behaviours among more marginalised populations and to encourage them to visit a GP if they have symptoms.

Other indicators of the quality of Danish primary care present a mixed picture

Another guide to the quality of primary care can be seen in the prescribing behaviour of GPs. Danish GPs fare well compared with others when it comes to prescribing diabetic patients with cholesterol-lowering medication to prevent cardiovascular events (Figure 2.9). Almost 80% of these patients are prescribed this medication, as recommended in clinical guidelines.

Danish GPs also compare well on the potentially harmful practice of prescribing elderly patients with long-term benzodiazepines (Figure 2.10), although the low rates in the Netherlands and Finland suggest this can be improved. Benzodiazepines are associated with adverse effects in elderly people. A 2007 study estimated there were some 100 000 benzodiazepine-dependent patients in Denmark, accounting for about 2% of the population (Jørgensen, 2007).

Denmark has made concerted efforts to reduce benzodiazepine prescribing. An intervention trialled in one municipality, involving ten Danish medical practices, produced encouraging results. As part of the intervention, a prescription for benzodiazepines could be issued for only one month at a time, and only following consultation. Fifteen months after the intervention began, the use of benzodiazepine-hypnotics declined by

46.5%, and the use of benzodiazepine-anxiolytics by 41.7%. This was done without any serious side effects observed in the patients in whom the drug was reduced (Jørgensen, 2007). This simple intervention could serve as a guide for other municipalities to consider. It could also be useful for other countries, particularly Portugal and Norway, which each have very high rates of prescribing of benzodiazepines.

Figure 2.9. People with diabetes with a prescription of cholesterol-lowering medication in the past year, 2013 (or nearest year)

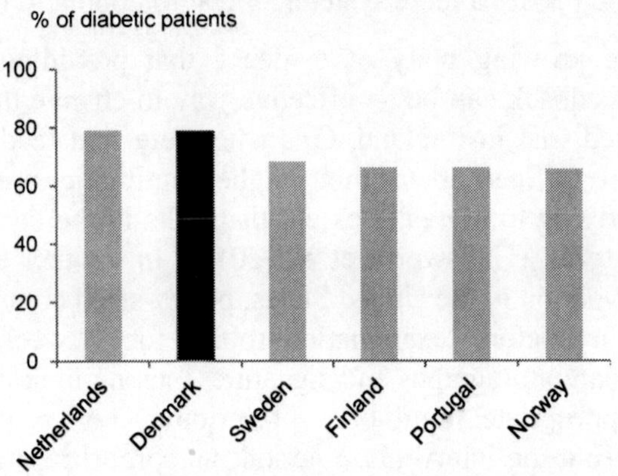

Source: OECD Health Statistics 2016, http://dx.doi.org/10.1787/health-data-en.

Figure 2.10. Elderly patients prescribed long-term benzodiazepines or related drugs, 2013 (or nearest year)

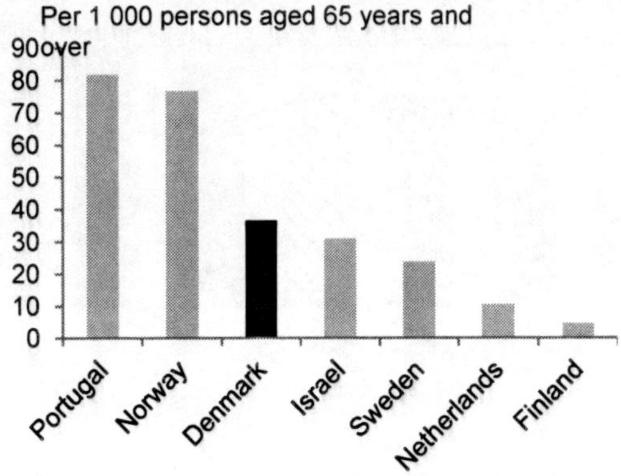

Source: OECD Health Statistics 2016, http://dx.doi.org/10.1787/health-data-en.

Danish GPs perform moderately well when it comes to antibiotic use, although they prescribe them more frequently than GPs in the Netherlands and Sweden (Figure 2.11). Much of this prescribing appears to be inappropriate. For example, in a recent OECD policy survey on waste in health systems, Denmark reported that treatment for upper respiratory tract infections accounts for 20% to 30% of total antibiotic consumption. The use of antibiotics for upper respiratory tract infections is not recommended, as it is potentially harmful without providing effective treatment against the infection. It may also contribute to antibiotic resistance, which poses a more systemic threat to population health.

There is a growing body of evidence that providing doctors with personalised feedback can be an effective way to change their behaviour. In a randomised trial in England, GPs who were sent feedback from the Chief Medical Officer about their higher antibiotic prescribing rates reduced prescribing to a greater extent than GPs in the control group not given the feedback (Hallsworth et al., 2016). In another example of an effective intervention in the United States, poster-sized commitment letters were posted in doctors' examination rooms for 12 weeks. The letters featured clinician photographs and signatures, stating their commitment to avoiding inappropriate antibiotic prescribing for acute respiratory infections. During the intervention period, inappropriate prescribing rates increased from 43.5% to 52.7% for the control group, but decreased from 42.8% to 33.7% in the intervention group (Meeker et al., 2014).

Figure 2.11. Overall volume of antibiotics prescribed, 2013 (or nearest year)

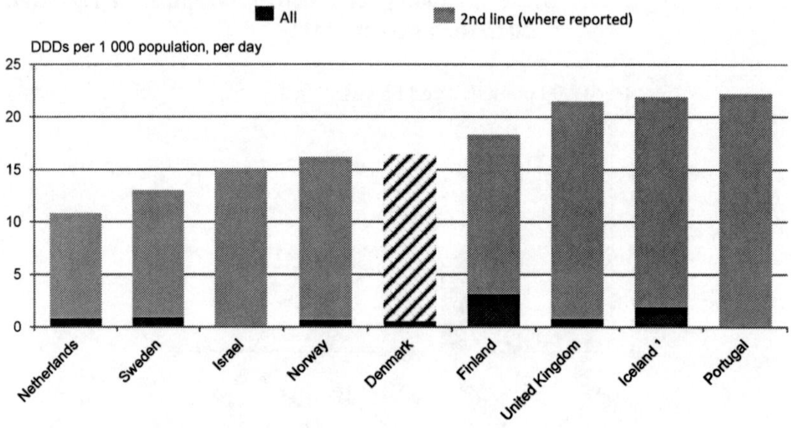

1. Data refer to all sectors (not only primary care).

Source: European Centre for Disease Prevention and OECD Health Statistics 2016, http://dx.doi.org/10.1787/health-data-en.

In other indicators of quality in primary care, Denmark should be commended for its efforts to increase the influenza vaccination coverage among people aged 65 and over (Figure 2.12). Coverage more than doubled from 20% in 2003, to 46% in 2013 – the largest rise compared with selected countries (OECD, 2015). Denmark makes influenza vaccinations free for people aged 65 and older. The rise in coverage, which is largely due to public education campaigns, is all the more striking given that some countries, including the Netherlands, Sweden and Finland, have experienced a declining trend. However, coverage is still well short of the World Health Assembly target of at least 75% of the elderly population by 2010, a target that the United Kingdom has achieved.

Figure 2.12. Influenza vaccination coverage, population aged 65 and over, 2003-13 (or nearest period)

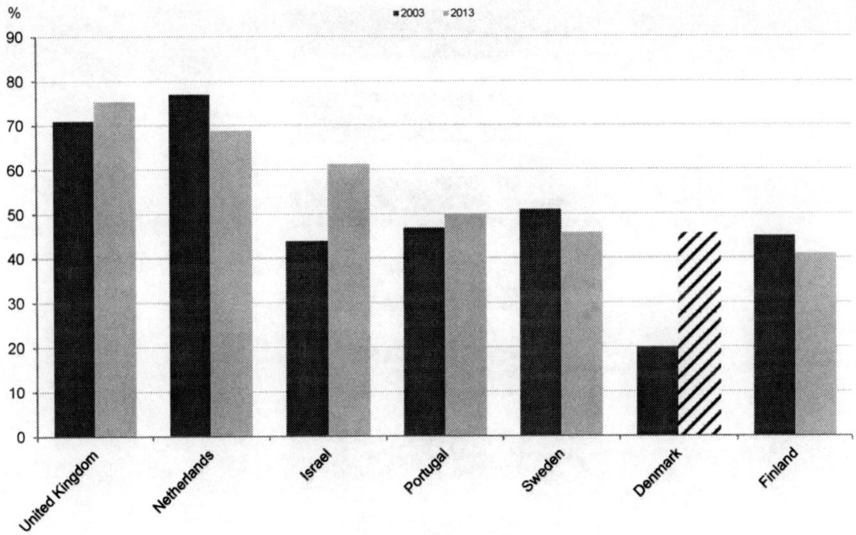

Source: OECD Health Statistics 2016, http://dx.doi.org/10.1787/health-data-en.

By contrast, Denmark needs to strengthen crucial public health programmes such as childhood vaccination. Coverage for measles vaccination is of particular concern as, at 89%, it stands well below the OECD average of 94% (Figure 2.13). It is also well below selected comparable countries, which have all achieved coverage above 90%. In the case of Portugal, 98% of children are vaccinated (OECD Health Statistics, 2016).

While measles has been rare in Denmark in recent years, there was a large outbreak in the country in January 2011 connected with a larger European outbreak that was the continent's most substantial in 15 years (Danish Health and Medicines Authority, 2013). The outbreak highlights that countries cannot afford to be complacent and allow vaccination rates to slide, as measles continues to pose a serious and potentially fatal threat to population health. Given that measles vaccinations are free and usually carried out by GPs in Denmark, there is a strong role for GPs to play in educating patients that the measles vaccination is safe, effective and potentially life-saving.

Figure 2.13. Vaccination against measles, children aged 1, 2013

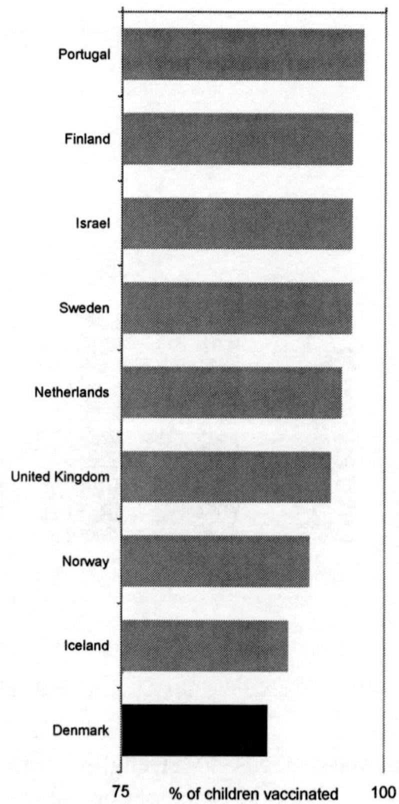

Source: WHO/UNICEF.

A range of initiatives aim to strengthen the quality of Danish primary care

Mandatory primary care accreditation is a relatively new quality improvement tool introduced in Denmark as part of 2014 agreement with PLO. Implementation began in January 2016, and each general practice has three years to be accredited in accordance with the Danish Quality Model (*Den Danske Kvalitetsmodel*, DDKM) – the general accreditation system for all health care providers including hospitals and pharmacies. The Danish Institute for Quality and Accreditation in Healthcare (IKAS) develops and runs the Danish accreditation programme for health care providers. The Danish regions give each practice 10 000 kroner at the beginning of the accreditation process, and a further 10 000 kroner once they have gained accreditation. These sums cover the entire cost of the accreditation process, so there is not a financial disincentive against accreditation. As at January 2016, 1 820 general medicine practices were clients of IKAS (IKAS, 2016).

The model recognises three types of quality: clinical, organisational and patient-perceived quality. These are covered by 16 standards (Box 2.3).

The standards were developed by a group representing the Association of General Practitioners (PLO), the Danish College of General Practitioners (DSAM), the Danish regions, and IKAS. Clinical quality is monitored and developed through the use of International Classification of Primary Care (ICPC) coding, and statistics regarding the use of medicine. Practices must also work with national or regional guidelines where they exist, to ensure that doctors and other staff keep their professional knowledge updated. Quality should also have been monitored through reports from the DAMD quality indicators database. However, the DAMD database has been dissolved and no alternative has been established so far. Consequently, quality monitoring in primary care is seriously hampered.

Box 2.3. Standards for general practice accreditation

1. Professional quality
2. Clinical quality
3. Avoidable adverse events (such as medication errors resulting from a prescriber's failure to consult a patient's medical record)
4. Patient experience
5. Prevention of mistakes regarding patients' identity
6. Handling of medicines and repeated prescriptions
7. Laboratory and imaging investigations
8. Basic life support after cardiac arrest
9. Handling of patient journals and data security
10. Access (includes physical access such as for people with disabilities, as well as access to health services – standard requirements as set in the agreement with the regions and possibility for online booking of a consultation and minimum one day per week access outside normal working hours.)
11. Referrals (does the GP follow the right designated patient pathway for referrals, such as to hospitals and community care)
12. Co-ordination of patient pathways/disease management
13. Acquisition, storage, and disposal of medical supplies
14. Hygiene
15. Management
16. Employment, introduction of new personnel and competency development.

Source: http://www.ikas.dk/.

Organisational quality focuses on ensuring the continuity of patient pathways. It should be informed by feedback from patients, such as patient evaluations, as well as data on referrals and drug prescribing. Each practice must develop procedures for learning based on feedback for the purpose of quality improvement. Patient-perceived quality is monitored and developed through patient evaluations that should be conducted at least every third year, as well as a review of complaints.

In another initiative aimed at improving quality, Regional Consultative Committees (*Sundhedskoordinationsudvalg*) exist in every region, and are mandatory under the Health Act. These committees consist of elected officials from the region, the municipalities within the region and local GPs. The committees support the quality and co-ordination of care between the primary and secondary sector, and one of their tasks is to develop the framework of health care agreements between the regions and municipalities. They also set goals for the development of health care in the region, follow up on the implementation of the health care agreements, and evaluate the regional health care plan.

Each region also has its own quality organisation, which comprises GPs and regional staff and engages in initiatives to improve quality and safety, and provides continuing education to the GPs. To ensure that doctors' skills are up to date, it is mandatory for GPs to participate in "systematic continuing education". This consists of five themes in primary care considered most important in terms of GP skill development. This includes chronic disease, mental health and elderly patients. GPs must participate in three days of this education each year, and are compensated a maximum of 4 500 kroner per day for their participation.

Danish patients appear to be satisfied with the quality of primary care

Every third year, Danish GPs have to evaluate their patients' satisfaction with the care they provide using the DANPEP survey. This questionnaire is a Danish version of the EUROPEP survey for patient evaluation of general practice. Patients are asked about their relationship with their doctor, their medical care, information and support, the organisation of services, and accessibility. GPs receive feedback on their results. The new primary care accreditation standards include a requirement that GPs must evaluate patient experience.

Previous DANPEP results have found high levels of satisfaction overall. An evaluation using EUROPEP suggests a positive GP assessment is strongly associated with increasing patient age and increasing frequency of attendance. Patients with a chronic condition were more positive, but poor self-rated health was strongly associated with less positive scores (Heje et al., 2008). Another study based on the EUROPEP survey found more patients reported worries about their health, unmet expectations and dissatisfaction with their GP after consultation when no diagnosis was made, compared with patients who received a diagnosis. Patient dissatisfaction was mostly related to the medical examination and GP explanations (Rosendal et al., 2016).

In addition, the National Survey of Patient Experience (LUP) is conducted annually on behalf of the five regions. While the focus is on the country's hospitals, it also includes a question assessing how well co-ordinated the patient's care was between the primary and secondary care sectors: "What is your assessment of how well the unit informed your general practitioner about your patient pathway (examination/treatment)?" The 2006 survey found that 78.5% responded positively to that question. There was also significant variation between hospitals on that indicator, with a difference of 24.3% between the highest and lowest ranking hospitals (Unit of Patient Evaluation, 2006). Comparable questions on co-ordination between primary and secondary care were not asked in later LUP surveys.

When compared with other countries, Danish family doctors rate highly. In a European Commission Special Eurobarometer survey, 91% of Danish people gave a positive assessment of the quality of family doctors or GPs, compared with a European Union average of 84%. This was the fifth-highest ranking in the survey. Denmark also performed strongly on the question of affordability, with only 1% of people saying it was not very affordable or not at all affordable, compared with a European Union average of 11%. However, on the question of availability and access to family doctors or GPs, only 82% responded access was easy, lower than the European Union average of 88% (European Commission, 2007).

With the collapse of the Danish General Practice Database, however, information on quality of care is now much more limited

Danish authorities collect substantial amounts of data about general practice activity. This information, however, is limited in its usefulness, as it presents only a picture of the volume and costs of activity. This means that while it is possible to know why patients visit a GP, the quality and outcomes of the services they receive remains unclear.

This limited transparency means that GPs and the authorities that pay for primary care are often unable to understand the value of Danish primary care. The absence of this information means GPs cannot use data to drive improvements in their clinical practice, with their patients the principal beneficiaries of this analysis.

Denmark has been one of the world leaders in the use of health data. Primary care is the only part of the Danish health system where this information void exists. This situation lies in contrast with Danish hospitals, where specialists are publicly employed and required to report data related to quality of care on a range of indicators and diseases, and the data are systematically collected and publicly reported.

As outlined in Section 1.3, this situation has largely come about due to the demise of the Danish General Practice Database (DAMD). Compounding the situation is that Danish general practice is predominantly private sector, even though it is publicly funded. This makes it more challenging to demand that GPs provide data on the quality of their care. There may be some reluctance on the part of GPs to provide the data due to fears it will be used for performance measurement, and in pay-for-performance schemes.

Of most concern is the impact the lack of information has on patients, if it means they cannot access information about their own health. The DAMD system previously enabled them to obtain information about their diagnosis, prescriptions and laboratory results. While there are other means patients can use to see information about their prescriptions and laboratory results, patients can no longer view information about their diagnosis and laboratory tests analysed in GP practice. In addition, GPs no longer have access to the patient overviews that many used to track patient care and provide reminders for recommended follow-up on things such as chronic disease management and vaccinations.

Schroll et al. (2012) demonstrate how useful such data can be for quality improvement. They found the collection of electronic data from general practice, and providing GPs with feedback with reports on quality of care for diabetes patients, reduced the proportion of type 2 diabetes patients with no medication, despite values for HbA1c, blood pressure, and cholesterol levels above target levels. A limitation of the study, however, is the lack of a control group, so it is difficult to draw direct causal inferences.

Patient involvement and representation in the health system could be improved

Health policy makers are increasingly recognising the importance of person-centred care, and delivering health services that are responsive to patients' needs. This means delivering effective and appropriate care close to where people live. In the case of patients with chronic disease in particular, this means a multidisciplinary team of health workers providing care that is seamless, to reduce the risk of duplication and errors that can result from poor care co-ordination.

A crucial part of person-centred care is giving patients the tools they need to play an active role in making decisions about their health care. Denmark is a forerunner in making data more accessible and more comprehensible to patients through the website *sundhed.dk*. The portal is a single digital space where Danish citizens can find information on waiting times, patient satisfaction and a range of quality indicators, as well as access their (almost) fully comprehensive health records – National Health record. As described earlier, the lack of data sharing from GP sector following the collapse of DAMD is, however, a major setback to this otherwise very innovative system.

There is still scope, however, for patients to play a more substantial role in making decisions about their care. Clinicians need to be trained and supported to understand not only patient symptoms, but also their values and preferences, and how they can empower patients to be more involved. They need to be equipped with the skills to communicate with patients knowledge about their condition, what they can do to engage in self-management, and where they can get more information about their condition. Among the tools that can facilitate dialogue between clinicians and patients is decision aids. These tools help patients make decisions about the benefits, risks and costs of treatment alternatives.

Denmark is developing “patient plans” for people diabetes, COPD and rheumatic disease as part of a collaboration between the government, Danish regions and Local Government Denmark that began in 2015. The plans aim to give patients with these conditions a better understanding of their treatment and promote self-management. The plan is jointly created by the patient and the GP, with a focus on the patient’s needs, motivation and resources. Patients will eventually be able to access their plan electronically. The plans have not yet been implemented, but it is important to note that success will depend on clinicians being trained and supported in regularly using them, and seeing their value.

Social inequalities can be a major barrier to patient participation, and can be challenging to overcome. People with lower levels of education can find it more difficult to understand health information. There is a need for strategies to strengthen health literacy to help these patients be more involved. The Danish Government has developed 11 booklets on subjects including alcohol, physical activity and mental health. A health promotion centre was also set up, with a team of people helping to implement the recommendations of the booklets. However, a more proactive approach would include developing education programmes tailored to specific vulnerable population groups to boost health literacy and provide information about both prevention of disease and self-management.

Obtaining information directly from patients can be instructive in determining what their needs are. Patient-Reported Experience Measures (PREMs) seek the perspective of patients about their experience based on the process of care, and are used in Denmark in both hospitals and primary care. Patient-Reported Outcome Measures (PROMs) assess a patient's outcomes, such as whether they are experiencing less pain after surgery, and other aspects of quality of life. They are used to a lesser extent in health systems.

The use of PROMs is more straightforward in patients who have had surgery, in that a patient's quality of life is measured before and after a surgical intervention. The use of PROMs in chronic disease is more difficult, as there are numerous methodological questions that remain unresolved. However, their use in patients with chronic disease would be very valuable in gaining an understanding of the quality of life of these patients.

Denmark collects PROMs data in seven of its more than 60 clinical registries, mostly for the purpose of shared decision making between patients and clinicians to improve patient outcomes. However, while there is a move towards a national PROMs programme for all hospital inpatient and ambulatory care, it has not been determined whether general practice will be part of this. It should be, in recognition that general practice is a vital part of the health system, and knowing the outcomes of patients in primary care is arguably even more important, as it can demonstrate how well patients fare after using primary care services, and how well primary care is keeping them out of hospital. The use of PROMs in general practice is something that could be discussed as part of the negotiation for the next agreement with PLO.

Among the clinical registers already collecting PROMs is the one for arthritis, which shows promise in how it can help improve patients' quality of life. PROMs data reported by a patient can be looked up by their doctor and compared with other clinical data to assess, for example, if a patient is in more pain, finds it difficult to walk, and requires adjustments to their medication. The doctor enters the clinical findings into the database and, when the patient returns, the process is repeated. The doctor compares the data with the data from the previous consultation to determine if there have been improvements. This use of PROMs has great potential in helping doctors and patients make decisions about treatment. In order for it to be effective, doctors and patients need to be educated as to the usefulness of the information, and clinicians need to be trained in how to interpret and use the data.

2.3. The efficiency and financial sustainability of primary care

Danish GPs' salaries are increasing, but volumes of activity appear stable

The income of Danish GPs is 2.7 times the average national wage, according to data submitted to the OECD. With the exception of Germany, this is broadly in line with GP incomes in other health systems where self-employment is the dominant contractual model (Figure 2.14). The trajectory of GPs' incomes can be compared within the same set of countries. The comparison of trend lines reveals that GP incomes in Denmark have been rising at broadly the same rate as self-employed GPs in other health systems, such as France and Belgium. GP incomes in some health systems, notably the United Kingdom and the Netherlands have actually been falling (Figure 2.15; OECD Health Statistics, 2016).

Figure 2.14. Self-employed GPs' income as compared with average wage, 2014 (or the nearest year)

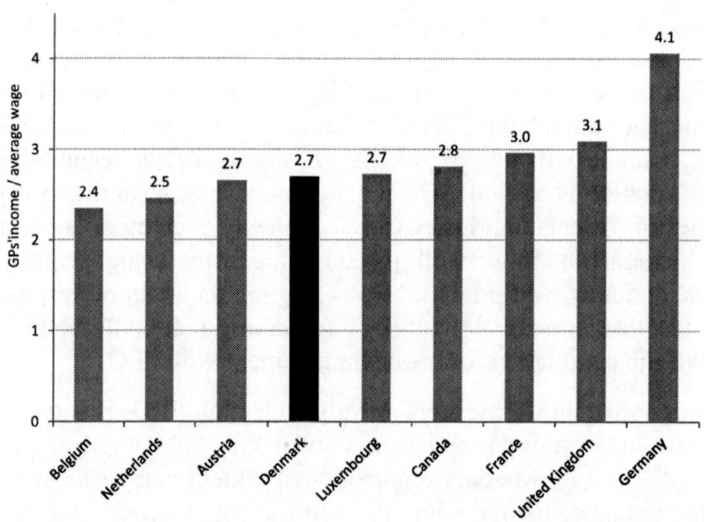

Note: Data for Denmark, France and Germany is for 2011.

Source: OECD Health Statistics 2016, http://dx.doi.org/10.1787/health-data-en.

Figure 2.15. Trends in self-employed GPs' income, 2002-14 (or nearest period)

USD PPP

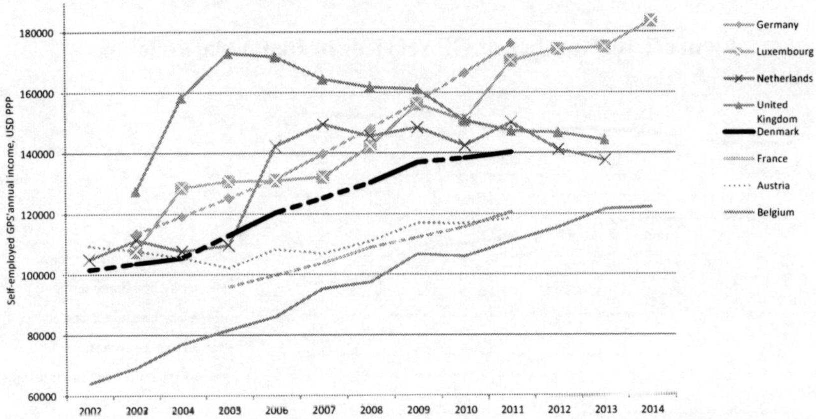

Note: Annual income before tax and other deductions but less of practice costs. For Denmark, France, and Germany dashed line indicates break in data series - income was estimated based on the available data.

Source: OECD Health Statistics 2016, http://dx.doi.org/10.1787/health-data-en.

The overall volume of GP activity in Denmark, however, appears to be relatively stable over the past decade. The total number of consultations rose rising slightly from 36.0 million (including preventive services) in 2006 to 37.8 million in 2014. Daytime consultations rose by 1.6 million between 2006 and 2014 (less than 10%). Taking into account population growth and changes in the age structure, this is not a substantial rise. An interesting trend is that telephone consultations declined by 24% during that period, while there were ten times as many email consultations, suggesting some of the patients who previously might have called their doctor are opting for email (Figure 2.16).

Of particular concern is the decline in preventive services of 36% (from 1.4 million to less than 900 000), at a time when the country's burden of chronic disease is high and poised to rise further. The fact that Denmark has a high prevalence with regards to risk factors such as smoking, alcohol and obesity (Figures 1.4 to 1.7) is also indicative of the need for preventive activities to be strengthened. GPs have an important role to play in this, in identifying patients at risk and in identifying those with poor health literacy who need extra support. While the fee-for-service payment system for GPs does include an item for preventive services, the fact that there is a decline in these activities suggests the incentive is not sufficient, or well-enough designed, to encourage GPs to invest time on prevention.

Figure 2.16. Number of GP services in Denmark, 2006-14

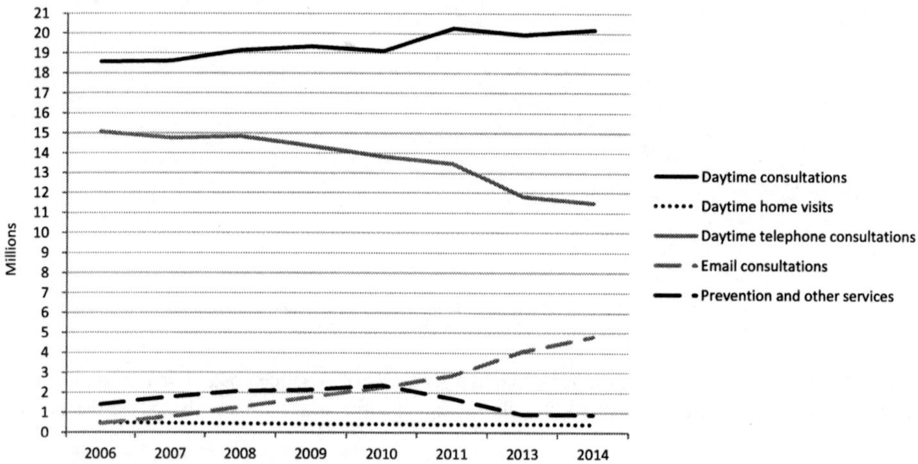

Note: 2012 has been excluded due to some missing data.

Source: Statistics Denmark, https://www.dst.dk/en.

Variations can be detected in the volume of GPs activity, in ways inversely related to need

OECD analysis of data from Danish National Health Profile reveals that in the municipalities that harbour the biggest percentage of the least healthy citizens have the lowest rates of regular primary care consultation. The use of the word "regular" instead of "frequent" is intentional, as the data at the municipality level provides the percentage of inhabitants that have seen a GP at least once in the last year. Indicators in Danish National Health Profile are based on a survey of representative sample of around 300 000 Danes, repeated every three years. The least healthy citizens are those whose score on questions about physical health belongs to the lowest 10% of the population's scores. These questions address self-assessed health and limitations in mobility and activities of daily life, as well as the prevalence of pain and other long-term conditions. Analysis of data on contact to a GP and population health, as measured by the distribution of the least healthy citizens across municipalities, reveals certain geographical trends illustrated in Figure 2.17.

Figure 2.17 divides Danish municipalities into nine clusters according to population health (best 1, medium 2 and worst 3) and regularity of contacts to GPs (most A, medium B and least regular C). In addition, each cluster includes information on average population density in the municipalities belonging to it. For example, most Danes belong to cluster B2, with medium population health and medium regularity of contacts to GPs, containing both densely and sparsely populated municipalities.

Figure 2.17. Danish municipalities organised with respect to health status, regularity of general-practitioner contacts, and density of population

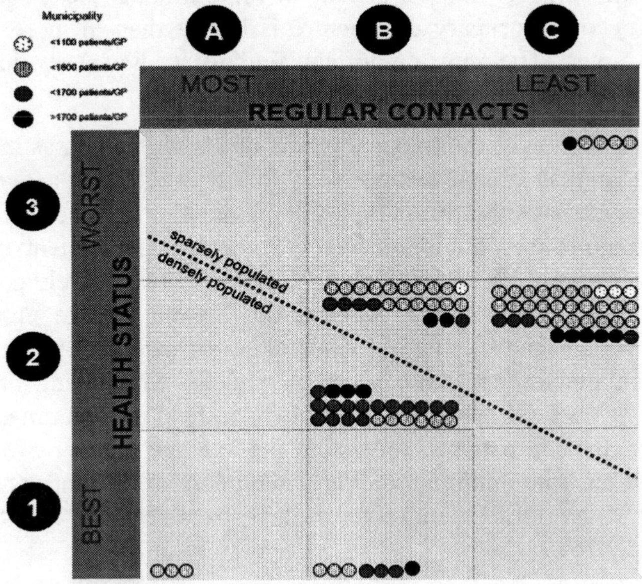

Note: Nine clusters according to population health (best 1, medium 2 and worst 3) and regularity of contacts to GPs (most A, medium B and least regular C). In each cluster, the number of dots corresponds to the number of municipalities belonging to it, with the colour of a dot indicating average number of patients per GP in this municipality. Moreover, municipalities are divided into densely and sparsely populated, as indicated by the dashed line.

Source: OECD analysis of data from Danish National Health Profile (2013), Statistics Denmark (2015), and Danish regions (2015).

Including information on population density reveals that the worst health outcomes are concentrated in less populated areas – cluster C3. This is also where the least regular GP contacts can be found. Inversely, the municipalities with the best health are in the densely populated areas

– clusters A1 and B1. This is also where the most regular contacts to GPs can be found – cluster A1. This indicates that the use of GPs services is inversely related to health needs of the population.

It is not, however, the case that there are systematically more patients per doctor in the most remote areas – the share of municipalities with an average number of patients per doctor exceeding 1 700 is comparable between the densely and sparsely populated areas. Moreover, in the less populated part of the country there are many more municipalities where the average number of patients per GP is below the threshold of 1 600 patients. Thus, one possible explanation for the differences in regularity of contacts to GPs is that in remote areas the distance (or travel time) to the primary care centre is longer than in more densely populated areas. The most important finding is, however, that there appear to be unmet population health needs.

The distribution of the frequency of contacts with a GP, as measured by average number of contacts per year, follows a different geographical pattern. Danish patients contact their GP on average 7.5 times per year in 2013. Maximum and minimum average contacts per patient in a GP practice were 3 and 13, respectively (SSI, 2015).[1] The densely populated Capital Region, for example, features the lowest average number of visits per patient, but the highest percentages of patients that have seen their general practitioner in the past year. This fits with having a high GP density, with each GP having many patients to tend to. The same pattern is seen for diabetic patients, for whom the average number of contacts was almost 16, with minimum of 7 and maximum of 26 contacts in 2013 (SSI, 2015 and OECD analysis of data from Danish Health Data Authority, 2016).

It cannot be excluded that the geographical variations described reflect weaknesses in the quality and/or organisational structure of the Danish primary care sector. In any case, primary care providers, led by GPs, are the group of health professionals most suited to address any geographical or socio-economic disparities in health and use of health care services. However, the current weaknesses in the data infrastructure underpinning the delivery, monitoring and evaluation of primary care make it extremely difficult to design appropriate actions to ensure an efficient distribution of activity and resources. Similarly, the FFS payment system, as described earlier makes it hard to understand exactly what is being done and to reward value appropriately.

Substantial geographical variations exist on quality indicators

Geographical variations are also revealed in a number of quality indicators for primary care such as avoidable hospital admission for elderly, diabetes or COPD hospital admissions , as shown in Figure 2.18. The indicator on avoidable hospitalisations of elderly in this figure includes diagnoses that are widely recognised as frequently preventable and almost always treatable at the primary care level (dehydration, constipation, lower respiratory tract disease, cystitis, gastroenteritis, bride, nutrition anaemia, ulcer, and social care conditions). As discussed earlier, effective treatment at the primary care level could prevent hospitalisations for chronic conditions such as COPD or diabetes. Denmark appears to have room for improvement here, when compared with other OECD countries, including Nordic peers.

The rates of avoidable hospital admissions, as measured on the three indicators, vary substantially between regions; with Region Capital having more than 30% higher hospital admission rates than the best performing Region Southern Denmark, on all indicators. The indicators reveal even higher variation between municipalities in each region, with admissions positively correlated with population density and geographical proximity to a hospital. Preventable hospital admissions of the elderly vary from below 40 to above 90 per 1 000 elderly inhabitants in a municipality. Hospital admissions for COPD and diabetes patients also reveal close to two-fold variation between the group of the best and the group of the worst performing municipalities. There is however, a general trend of improvement as compared with situation in 2009.

As of 2013, Denmark has also collected also two indicators regarding rehabilitation at community facilities: median waiting time for rehabilitation and the share of rehabilitation plans that are prepared within a recommended time-limit. At regional level, the median waiting time varied little, between 13 and 16 days. Larger variations exist at the municipal level, with waiting time in almost half of the municipalities exceeding 14 days and in some reaching 40 days in 2015. There are also no apparent improvements since 2013. Regarding the share of rehabilitation plans prepared within a recommended time-limit, variations are much smaller with rates generally close to 90% across all municipalities in 2015.

Figure 2.18. Avoidable hospital admissions of elderly, COPD hospital admissions and diabetes hospital admissions by region, age and gender standardised, 2015

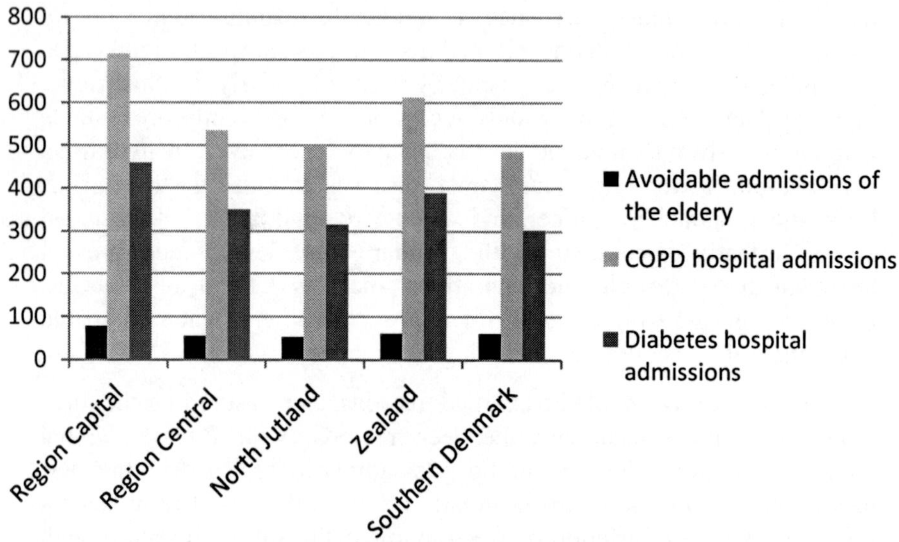

Note: Avoidable hospital admission of elderly are per 1 000 elderly inhabitants. COPD hospital admissions are per 1 000 inhabitants with COPD. Diabetes hospital admissions are per 1 000 inhabitants with diabetes.

Source: Indblik i Sundhedsvæsenet Resultater (2016).

In 2014, the Ministry of Health decided to dedicate DKK 900 million to initiatives targeting long waiting times for rehabilitation, for the period 2015 to 2018. The overreaching aim was to lower median waiting times in municipalities to 14 days or less (*Aftale om satspuljen på sundheds- og ældreområdet* for 2016-19). There was, however, lack of agreement between KL and Danish regions on how to implement this state initiative. In consequence, no progress in the area has been made to date.

These indicators suggest potential for improvement in the efficiency of Danish primary care, particularly with regards to the articulation between GP services and municipality-led services, such as rehabilitation. The development of performance indicators in Denmark's community care sector is promising, illustrating an awareness of the need to monitor and improve performance in this area. The GP sector, however, risks lagging behind even as compared with the community providers, if the issues of transparency and accountability are not resolved.

Regarding the global primary health care budget in Denmark, total expenditure on GP services reached approximately DKK 8.5 billion in 2015, out of which DKK 5 billion was activity-based. Between 2005 and 2015, the activity-based spending has been growing by 1.5% annually adjusting for inflation. At least half of this expansion can be accounted for by the population growth and the increasing share of elderly citizens. The other half can be due to higher volume of more expensive services as compared to earlier years.

In order to improve control of spending, total expenditure on GP services are subject to a global ceiling since 2011. The activity and the corresponding expenditures are monitored on quarterly basis and GP practices receive alerts when activity levels/expenditures are nearing the ceiling. Expenditure ceilings, or global budget caps, are in place across most OECD health systems. Although the policy may be unpopular with some patient groups or health care providers, it is an entirely reasonable policy to maintain.

The Danish primary care sector is, however, not subject to the so-called "standard efficiency requirement", which has been applied to the hospital sector in Denmark for several decades. The efficiency requirement means that each hospital is expected to achieve 2% productivity gains annually. In other words, each hospital is expected to achieve 2% increase in activity without a corresponding increase in funding. It might, however, prove difficult to embark on a necessary range of quality improving initiatives, especially in the area of care for the vulnerable elderly, without engaging further resources. For example, there is a clear need to adjust GP remuneration system such that it better reflects the workload related to management of patients with chronic conditions, which can be difficult within the current financial framework.

Note

1. Contacts include all modes of day consultations, including telephone and e-mail consultations. numbers are calculated for patients who saw their GP at least once in 2013.

References

Allemani, C. et al. and the CONCORD Working Group (2014), "Global Surveillance of Cancer Survival 1995–2009: Analysis of Individual Data for 25 676 887 Patients from 279 Population-based Registries in 67 Countries (CONCORD-2)", *The Lancet*, published online 26 Nov. 2014, http://dx.doi.org/10.1016/S0140-6736(14)62038-9.

Berchet, C. and C. Nader (2016), "The Organisation of Out-of-Hours Primary Care in OECD Countries", *OECD Health Working Paper*, No. 89, OECD Publishing, Paris, http://dx.doi.org/10.1787/5jlr3czbqw23-en.

Bourgueil, Y., A. Marek and J. Mousquès (2005), "The Participation of Nurses in Primary Care in Six European Countries, Ontario and Quebec", *Issues in Health Economics Analysis*, Health Economics Letter No. 95, Institute for Information in Health Economics, Paris.

Bunn, F., G. Byrne and S. Kendall (2004), "Telephone Consultation and Triage: Effects on Health Care Use and Patient Satisfaction (Review)", *Cochrane Database of Systematic Reviews*, Vol. 3, Art. No.: CD004180.

Christensen, M.B. and F. Olesen (1998), "Out of Hours Service in Denmark: Evaluation Five Years After Reform", *British Medical Journal*, Vol. 316, pp. 1502–1505, http://dx.doi.org/10.1136/bmj.316.7143.1502.

Coleman, M.P. et al. (2011), "Cancer Survival in Australia, Canada, Denmark, Norway, Sweden, and the UK, 1995–2007 (the International Cancer Benchmarking Partnership): An Analysis of Population-based Cancer Registry Data", *The Lancet*, Vol. 377, No. 9760, pp. 127-138, http://dx.doi.org/10.1016/S0140-6736(10)62231-3.

Dale, J. et al. (2004), "Safety of Telephone Consultation for 'Non-serious' Emergency Ambulance Service Patients", *Quality & Safety in Health Care*, Vol. 13, No. 5, pp. 363-373.

Danish Health and Medicines Authority (2013), *Denmark's Childhood Vaccination Programme,* 7th edition, Copenhagen.

Derkx, H.P. et al. (2008), "Quality of Clinical Aspects of Call Handling at Dutch Out of Hours Centres: Cross Sectional National Study", *British Medical Journal,* Vol. 12, No. 337, a1264, http://dx.doi.org/10.1136/bmj.a1264.

European Commission (2007), *Special Eurobarometer: Health and Long-term Care in the European Union.*

Flarup, L. et al. (2014), "Chronic-disease Patients and their Use of Out-of-hours Primary Health Care: A Cross-sectional Study", *BMC Family Practice*, Vol. 15, No. 114, http://dx.doi.org/10.1186/1471-2296-15-114.

Giesen, P. et al. (2007), "Safety of Telephone Triage in General Practitioner Cooperatives: Do Triage Nurses Correctly Estimate Urgency?", *Quality & Safety in Health Care*, Vol. 16, No. 3, pp. 181-184, http://dx.doi.org/10.1136/qshc.2006.018846.

Guldbrandt, L.M. et al. (2015), "The Role of General Practice in Routes to Diagnosis of Lung Cancer in Denmark: A Population-based Study of General Practice Involvement, Diagnostic Activity and Diagnostic Intervals", *BMC Health Services Research*, Vol. 15:21, http://dx.doi.org/10.1186/s12913-014-0656-4.

Hallsworth, M. et al. (2016), "Provision of Social Norm Feedback to High Prescribers of Antibiotics in General Practice: A Pragmatic National Randomised Controlled Trial", *The Lancet*, Vol. 387, No. 10029, pp. 174-175.

Hansen, E.H. and S. Hunskaar (2011), "Telephone Triage by Nurses in Primary Care Out-of-hours Services in Norway: An Evaluation Study Based on Written Case Scenarios", *BMJ Quality & Safety*, Vol. 20, No. 5, pp. 390–396, http://dx.doi.org/10.1136/bmjqs.2010.040824.

Heje, H.N. et al. (2008), "Patient Characteristics Associated with Differences in Patients' Evaluation of their General Practitioner", *BMC Health Services Research*, Vol. 8:178, http://dx.doi.org/10.1186/1472-6963-8-178.

Huibers, L. et al. (2014), "Consumption in Out-of-hours Health Care: Danes Double Dutch?", *Scandinavian Journal of Primary Health Care*, Vol. 32, No. 1, pp. 44-50, http://dx.doi.org/10.3109/02813432.2014.898974.

Huibers, L. et al. (2011), "Safety of Telephone Triage in Out-of-hours Care: A Systematic Review", Vol. 29, No. 4, pp. 198-209, http://dx.doi.org/10.3109/02813432.2011.629150.

Hvidberg, L. et al. (2015), "Barriers to Healthcare Seeking, Beliefs about Cancer and the Role of Socio-economic Position. A Danish Population-based Study", *Preventive Medicine*, Vol. 71, pp. 107-113, http://dx.doi.org/10.1016/j.ypmed.2014.12.007.

IKAS – Danish Institute for Quality and Accreditation in Healthcare (2016), "Introduction to DDKM", *a*vailable at: http://www.ikas.dk/ddkm/ddkm-in-english/introduction-to-ddkm/ (accessed 03/06/2016).

Jensen, H., A. Nissen and P. Vedsted (2014), "Quality Deviations in Cancer Diagnosis: Prevalence and Time to Diagnosis in General Practice", *British Journal of General Practice*, Vol. 64, No. 619, pp. e92-e98, http://dx.doi.org/10.3399/bjgp14X677149.

Jørgensen, V.R. (2007), "An Approach to Reduce Benzodiazepine and Cyclopyrrolone Use in General Practice: A Study Based on a Danish Population", *CNS Drugs*, Vol. 21, No. 11, pp. 947-955.

Latter, S. et al. (2010), *Evaluation of Nurse and Pharmacist Independent Prescribing*, Department of Health Policy Research Programme Project 0160108, University of Southampton, Keele University.

Lattimer, V. et al. (1998), "Safety and Effectiveness of Nurse Telephone Consultation in Out-of-hours Primary Care: Randomised Controlled Trial", *British Medical Journal*, Vol. 317, No. 7165, pp. 1054-1059.

Lindblad, E. et al. (2010), "Experiences of the New Role of Advanced Practice Nurses in Swedish Primary Health Care – A Qualitative Study", *International Journal of Nursing Practice,* Vol. 16, No. 1, pp. 69-74, http://dx.doi.org/10.1111/j.1440-172X.2009.01810.x.

Meeker, D. et al. (2014), "Nudging Guideline-Concordant Antibiotic Prescribing: A Randomized Clinical Trial", *JAMA Internal Medicine*, Vol. 174, No. 3, pp. 425-431, http://dx.doi.org/10.1001/jamainternmed.2013.14191.

NHS – National Health Service (2016), "Urgent and Emergency Care Services in England", available at: http://www.nhs.uk/NHSEngland/AboutNHSservices/Emergencyandurgentcareservices/Pages/nhs-out-of-hours-services.aspx (accessed 09/06/2010).

Nørøxe, K.B. et al. (2013), "Could the Patient Have Been Seen by a Nurse; a Questionnaire-based Survey of GP and Patient Views in Danish General Practice", *BMC Family Practice*, Vol. 14:171, http://dx.doi.org/10.1186/1471-2296-14-171.

OECD (2015), *Health at a Glance 2015: OECD Indicators,* OECD Publishing, Paris, http://dx.doi.org/10.1787/health_glance-2015-en.

Pasini, A., G. Rigon and A. Vaona (2015), "A Cross-sectional Study of the Quality of Telephone Triage in a Primary Care Out-of-hours Service", *Journal of Telemedicine and Telecare*, Vol. 21, No. 2, pp. 68-72, http://dx.doi.org/10.1177/1357633X14566573.

PLO – Praktiserende Lægers Organisation (2013), "PLO Orientering – Nyt fra POL-Hovedstaden: Lægevagten i region Hovedstaden", Nr. 4, 25 April 2013.

Region Hovedstade – Enhed for Evaluering og Brugerinddragelse (2015), "Borgernes oplevelser af Akuttelefonen 1813: Telefonsurvey blandt 1.106 borgere, der har ringet til 1813", revised edition, 30 April 2015.

Rosendal, M. et al. (2016), "Symptoms as the Main Problem: A Cross-sectional Study of Patient Experience in Primary Care", *BMC Family Practice*, Vol. 17:29, http://dx.doi.org/10.1186/s12875-016-0429-8.

Schroll, H. et al. (2012), "The Danish Model for Improvement of Diabetes Care in General Practice: Impact of Automated Collection and Feedback of Patient Data", *International Journal of Family Medicine*, Vol. 2012, Article ID 208123, http://dx.doi.org/10.1155/2012/208123.

SSI (2015), *Synlighed om resultater i sundhedsvæsenet*, February.

Storm, H.H. et al. (2010), "Survival of Patients Diagnosed with Cancer in the Nordic Countries Up to 1999-2003 Followed to the End of 2006. A Critical Overview of the Results", *Acta Oncologica*, Vol. 49, No. 5, pp. 532-544, http://dx.doi.org/10.3109/02841861003801148.

Sundhedsstyrelsen (2009), *Kvaliteten i den danske lægevagtsordning*, December.

Unit of Patient Evaluation (2006), *Patients' Experiences in Danish Hospitals*, National Danish Survey of Patient Experiences, on behalf of the Danish Regions and the Danish Ministry of Interior and Health, available at: http://patientoplevelser.dk/files/dokumenter/artikel/survey_2006_english.pdf (accessed 01/06/2016).

Victorian Auditor-General (2010), *Delivery of Nurse-on-Call*, Victoria, Australia

ORGANISATION FOR ECONOMIC CO-OPERATION AND DEVELOPMENT

The OECD is a unique forum where governments work together to address the economic, social and environmental challenges of globalisation. The OECD is also at the forefront of efforts to understand and to help governments respond to new developments and concerns, such as corporate governance, the information economy and the challenges of an ageing population. The Organisation provides a setting where governments can compare policy experiences, seek answers to common problems, identify good practice and work to co-ordinate domestic and international policies.

The OECD member countries are: Australia, Austria, Belgium, Canada, Chile, the Czech Republic, Denmark, Estonia, Finland, France, Germany, Greece, Hungary, Iceland, Ireland, Israel, Italy, Japan, Korea, Latvia, Luxembourg, Mexico, the Netherlands, New Zealand, Norway, Poland, Portugal, the Slovak Republic, Slovenia, Spain, Sweden, Switzerland, Turkey, the United Kingdom and the United States. The European Union takes part in the work of the OECD.

OECD Publishing disseminates widely the results of the Organisation's statistics gathering and research on economic, social and environmental issues, as well as the conventions, guidelines and standards agreed by its members.

OECD PUBLISHING, 2, rue André-Pascal, 75775 PARIS CEDEX 16
(81 2017 02 1 P) ISBN 978-92-64-26944-6 – 2017

Achevé d'imprimer par Corlet Numérique - 14110 Condé-sur-Noireau
N° d'Imprimeur : 136889 - Dépôt légal : mars 2017 - *Imprimé en France*